How to Become a $uperstar $ales Professional

Prospecting and Solution-Based Selling Skills
for Business-to-Business Sales Professionals

WINNIE ARY

Cameo Publications, LLC

06 07 08 09 10 HH 5 4 3 2 1
First Edition
Printed in the United States of America
ISBN 10: 0-9774659-4-2
ISBN 13: 978-0-9774659-4-1
Bus058000 Business / Sales & Selling
Library of Congress Control Number: 2005938848
$18.95 U.S. Funds
$ 23.00 CAN Funds

Requests for permission to make copies of any part of this work can be made to:

Cameo Publications
478 Brown's Cove Road
Ridgeland, SC 29936

1-866-372-2636

Interior and Cover design by Cameo Publications, LLC.

"Effective Salespeople Are Essential . . . Not Optional!"

Dedication

To my brother Bruce—my hero. Fighting your own critical battle with cancer never kept you from being my number one fan and cheerleader during the writing of this book.

And

To my husband Earl, who continues to love and support me without qualification or reservation, and who provides the balance and stability in my life that is paramount to doing the work I love so much.

Contents

Acknowledgements   ix

Introduction   11

Do You Have What It Takes?   13

Prospecting and Developing New Business   23

Preparation and Attitude   29

Prospecting Skills   39

Making Contact and Gaining Attention   55

Ask for the Business   67

Addressing Objections and Resistance   77

The Touching Program   91

Listening and Asking Good Questions   103

Drills for Skills   115

Acknowledgements

Writing this book would have never happened without the support and encouragement of many people. I especially want to express my thanks to the following:

My Administrative Assistant, Angie Widmayer, who has been with me since 1989. Angie, I'm convinced that you were sent by God. Nothing could have happened without your attention to detail and unending support. The "good little Catholic girl" in you never stopped praying for the success of Ary Group and our clients.

Mike Gorman, former president of Thomas Ruff & Company; Joe Lozowski, President and CEO of Tangram Interiors; and Sandra Williams, Director of Dealer Development for S.P. Richard's, Co. You are three of my long-term clients, and I am eternally grateful for your years of continued support of my work and for the many doors you opened for me along the way. Mike, Joe, and Sandra, you always make me feel that I am part of your team rather than a paid consultant and trainer.

Dawn Josephson of Cameo Publications, who pushed me until I begged for mercy to ensure we met all our deadlines, crossed all the T's, and dotted all the I's. Dawn, her business partner David, and the staff at Cameo Publications exemplify the term "Superstar Professionals."

Introduction

What is a Superstar Sales Professional? What makes that person stand out in the crowd amongst other sales professionals?

The Superstar Sales Professional is consistently in the upper one-third of income earners on any sales team. Being successful may be their driving force, but the real report card is how much money they earn.

If they sell business equipment, industrial chemicals, office furniture, catering services, software applications, commercial printing, business insurance, or any one of hundreds of other products and services sold business-to-business today, the Superstar Sales Professional consistently earns more money than two-thirds of the sales team in their company.

Why so much emphasis on how much they earn? In sales driven organizations, sales is the focus, and when salespeople are selling well, they are making good money. When they are not selling well, everyone in the organization can be negatively affected.

Think about it: If a company sells a product or service to other businesses and sales are flat, that company is in trouble. Just look at the business section of the newspaper and you see it every day in bold print. When company sales are flat we see downsizing, wage freezes, benefit cuts, bankruptcy filings, and some even go out of business. To avoid putting everyone else in the company at risk, salespeople must perform well. And Superstar Sales Professionals do just that. They perform well.

Superstar Sales Professionals also take good care of existing customers. While they may not personally resolve customer service issues, Superstar Sales

Professionals make sure their customers are getting the service they deserve, and in a timely manner. They have impeccable follow-up and follow-through skills, and blaming someone else for things not getting done is not their style. They make things happen rather than waiting for things to happen.

Superstar Sales Professionals know the value of keeping existing customers satisfied. They know that existing customers are their greatest resource for referrals and repeat business. They also know that their customers buy from them because they trust them and feel that they know and understand their needs. As such, these superstars never allow existing customer relationships to go unattended.

Superstar Sales Professionals don't just talk about partnering with customers and clients; they make it happen. They make sure their customers view them as an asset to their business, not as an order takers.

Superstar Sales Professionals take the time to know enough about their customers or prospective customers to understand their needs and how to best position their products and services to not only win their business, but also keep their business. They focus on solution-based selling more than sales for the sake of sales.

Superstar Sales Professionals are team players, but not necessarily team focused. They interact well with co-workers and support staff, and they are true professionals. They do not bully or scream or yell. They treat others with respect.

Superstar Sales Professionals are good developers of new business. They know the value and the need to make sure that new business efforts are timely, effective, and religiously performed. As such, Superstar Sales Professionals do not focus on filling their prospecting funnel; rather, they focus on never letting the funnel go empty.

So how can an average performing salesperson or a new to sales rookie become a Superstar?

Read on!

CHAPTER 1

Do You Have
What It Takes?

Q: What are the keys to becoming a Superstar Sales Professional?

A: Three things:

- Mindset
- Discipline
- Selling Skill

Do You Have the Superstar Sales Professional Mindset?

Before you can expect to become a Superstar Sales Professional, you must truly believe sales is an honorable and worthy profession. I'm always amazed how many salespeople genuinely believe that a successful sales career requires them to be overbearing and obnoxious. If salespeople do not achieve a high level of success, all too often they blame their lack of performance on their unwillingness to become that kind of person. Quite simply, they're dead wrong!

When I train salespeople, I often tease them about removing an evil spell they fell victim to sometime between the ages of 12 and 21. That's generally

13

when young people see or hear something that tells them "sales is disgusting and so are salespeople." So just in case you are suffering from that spell, let's get rid of it right now so we can move on.

ZAP! It's gone!!

Finally, that inaccurate belief and negative mindset about sales and salespeople are gone forever!

Before we removed the hex, you may have had a picture in your mind of how a salesperson looks and acts. Most likely, the image looked something like this:

> *A man sits at the dining room table in the home of an elderly couple. He has greasy, slicked back hair and wears a blue polyester suit about three sizes too small for him. He proudly displays gold chains around both wrists and his neck, and three huge gold rings on his fingers. He smells like cheap cologne. Beads of perspiration dance on his forehead and above his lip. He forcefully places a pen in the hands of the elderly gentleman and asks him to sign a bogus contract that will wipe out the couple's entire retirement savings.*

Are you laughing and nodding your head in agreement? I thought so. When I describe the previous image, people always tell me, "Winnie, that was exactly the picture I had in my mind, and I never wanted to be that kind of salesperson." But the man in the blue polyester suit is not a salesperson; he's a con artist. He bears no resemblance or relationship to the profile of a genuine Superstar Sales Professional.

If you are serious about becoming a Superstar Sales Professional, you must begin with a positive mindset about your chosen career. Until you do, you will be too afraid or uncomfortable to learn how to sell effectively. Your fear of looking or sounding like the man in the blue polyester suit will hold you back and prevent you from learning how to become a truly successful salesperson.

In the United States we may not have the largest population in the world or a monopoly on technology or natural resources. But we do have the greatest sales and marketing people. In fact, no one consistently sells their products and services as well as Americans. Just look at any major city in the world and you see American businesses everywhere: Coca-Cola, Fed Ex, McDonald's, and Microsoft, just to name a few. It's called professional selling, and it's an honorable profession.

Superstar Sales Professionals would never sell their customers a product or service that would not work for them, just to get a commission check. True salespeople honor and respect the commitments they make to their customers, to the company they represent, and to the support staff that assists them in processing the sale.

Superstar Sales Professionals focus on consultative and relationship selling. They make things happen that have a positive and lasting effect on our economy and on the quality of life in the United States, as well as around the globe. With this type of mindset guiding you, how can sales be anything less than honorable?

Do You Have Superstar Sales Discipline?

Superstar Sales Professionals have discipline, because without discipline, they can't be successful.

You must have discipline to practice your selling skills until they become as natural and spontaneous as brushing your teeth.

You must have discipline to schedule time for business development and never give up that time except for extreme emergencies.

You must have discipline to delegate non-revenue producing tasks to others and focus your energy and attention on the selling that Superstar Sales Professionals know always comes first.

You must have discipline to refuse to give away time when you know your return on investment is not worth it.

You must have discipline to make sure you've done everything you need to do to make a positive and lasting first impression on a prospective customer.

You must have discipline to break old habits that inhibit sales success and replace them with new ones that guarantee it.

You must have discipline to read a book or an article on a regular basis that will keep you at the cutting edge of what's happening in your industry and the world of business.

You must have discipline to become a
Superstar Sales Professional!

A number of years ago I discovered firsthand the importance of personal discipline and how it can affect your life, both personally and professionally.

I started my consulting and training business in 1988. Prior to that I had been successful, first in sales and then in sales management, and decided I wanted to go out on my own. Today, when people tell me how lucky I have been, I want to smack them!

Yes, I have a good business. I am a professional speaker, a business consultant, an author, and a trainer. However, none of that resulted from luck. My success came about through a combination of mindset, discipline, and skill. And in my case, when I was starting my business, discipline was number one.

Leaving my stable corporate position and starting a business out of my home seemed like a risky and even crazy venture. Remember, this was back in 1988. We were in the midst of a recession. Interest rates were at record levels, and money was tight. Such an environment seldom supported a high-risk venture, so I needed to be frugal and disciplined with both my money and my time.

I began the business at the dining room table. However, I quickly realized I needed to work in a room that actually looked like an office. I needed that kind of forced discipline to be successful.

Three days into building my business, I was in blue jeans and a sweatshirt tearing apart the upstairs guest bedroom. I tore down and stored the bed, the dresser, curtains, and even the family pictures, and replaced them with a card table, a folding metal chair, and a set of cheap Venetian blinds. If I were to succeed in my fledgling business, I needed a functional office.

Just a few months earlier, my husband Earl had turned a light shade of green when I broke the news that I wanted to resign my position and start my own company. We both knew the risks and the sacrifices my decision would mean. We agreed I would give it my best shot for one year to see if I could make the business work. If my best shot wasn't good enough, at the end of the year I would pull together a new resumé and look for a job.

We tightened our belts and gave up spending on things like dining out or vacations. We cut back on any unnecessary expenses in order to stretch our savings until my business was up and running. Making that happen depended on how much business I could find and how quickly I could find it. I needed business cards, letterhead, stationery, and some sort of brochure that explained who I was and what I had to offer.

After ten plus years in sales management, I was smart enough to know that mailing a vast quantity of brochures would generate a very low return on my investment. Advertising was very expensive, and even if I could afford it, what could I really say about myself at this point?

Sure, I could talk about what I had accomplished as a VP of Sales, but I could hardly brag about my track record as a consultant or a trainer, as I was still in the raw, start-up phase.

During the first few weeks of my new career, I could easily convince myself it was okay to do some laundry, start a roast for dinner, or just have an extra cup of coffee and read the paper in the morning. I soon realized I was developing bad habits that would sabotage my success from the very onset unless I took steps to break those habits immediately.

So developing a track record became my number one priority. And to do that I needed business. My focus had to be on finding opportunities and closing sales. Therefore, from that day on I decided *not* to engage in non-selling activities during peak selling hours unless I earned the time. It had to be a reward for something I had accomplished. Haircuts, shopping, personal telephone conversations, and non-urgent clerical and administrative paperwork did not take place between the hours of 8:30 a.m. and noon or between 1:00 p.m. and 4:00 p.m.

I decided to give myself an hour of free time during working hours only *as a reward for outstanding performance.* Outstanding performance meant making some great prospecting calls or getting an appointment with a qualified decision-maker. Rewards were not something I gave myself for staying focused on finding business, but rather for being *successful* at finding business.

I created a schedule that addressed day-by-day and hour-by-hour what I would be doing. Nothing was allowed to interfere with that schedule unless it was a family emergency or a revenue producing opportunity.

I did not do correspondence or set up files during peak prospecting hours. Instead, I focused my schedule on business development from 8:30 a.m. to noon, and again from 1:00 p.m. to 4:00 p.m. The rest of the time I worked on clerical and administrative tasks and on documenting what I had learned when making my prospecting calls.

In 1988, good contact management software was not readily available or affordable, so I used a homemade form with a box of index cards as a tickler file. I kept track of what was in my prospecting funnel on those index cards and used them to make sure I didn't miss the appropriate next step.

My day started in my office at the card table at 7:00 a.m. (I'm a morning person.) I allowed myself thirty minutes for lunch, which was usually when I put on the roast and threw in a tub of laundry or cleaned the cat's litter box. And I typically stopped working at 5:30 p.m. (I'm not good at working late.)

As the business grew, I adjusted my schedule, because I needed more time to take care of existing clients and developmental work, and I spent a little less time on prospecting. However, no month went by without some time being allocated for business development, a practice I still maintain today.

Did I ever cheat? You bet I did. And more often than I should have. However, the driving need to make a good living and find enough business to be successful always got me back on track.

Discipline is not about being perfect and doing everything right all the time. Discipline is about doing what you need to do to get yourself on track, keep yourself on track, or get yourself back on track when what you're doing is not working.

By the beginning of my second year, I had a "real" office in a business complex in Westerville, Ohio, close to home, complete with real office furniture (good-bye card table) and my name on the door. I also had an assistant, Angie, my angel sent by God, who is still with me today.

Ary Group has come a long way since those early days when I was tearing apart our guest bedroom to make that first office. But the lessons I learned back then about discipline and hard work continue to drive the business today and define its values.

A couple of years ago our neighborhood had a community garage sale to raise money for charity, so Earl and I looked for items in our basement to include. Stuck in a dark corner was that original old card table where my business had first seen the light of day. Earl suggested we throw it in with everything else we were unloading.

That conversation was one of our shorter ones! I quickly advised him that the card table was a family heirloom, and I was certain the children would fight over it after I was gone. "That's the table where Ary Group Incorporated was founded in January 1988," I told him. "End of discussion."

The card table reminded me of the discipline that had been necessary to get my business up and running. And I'm quite sure if we asked almost any Superstar Sales Professional, that person would tell you there was something similar he or she valued for the same reason.

Do You Have Superstar Sales Selling Skills?

As I mentioned earlier, Mindset, Discipline, and Selling Skills are the three key requirements of a Superstar Sales Professional. My many years in sales and sales management before starting my business gave me the right mindset. And discipline was right at the top of my "what I need to be successful" list.

Selling skills were the least of my concerns. I knew how to sell. Selling skills are as natural and spontaneous to me as breathing air. I don't even have to *think* about what to do in a selling situation; I *know* what to do. And my selling skills are where they need to be because I am, in a word, *brilliant*. I was a special child, born under a star, chosen by God to be a Superstar Sales Professional. (If you believe all that baloney, you will believe anything!)

Seriously, my selling skills are where they need to be because of hard work and practice. A "born" salesperson simply does not exist. Superstar Sales Professionals develop, fine-tune, and memorize good selling skills. They master a core set of competencies that when used at the appropriate time will almost always guarantee success.

When I say, "guarantee success," does that mean you will win every sale? Absolutely not. However, it does mean you will almost always do the right thing at the right time; and when you do lose, the reason will not be a lack of selling skills.

So many salespeople just simply "make it up" as they go along. They "wing it" and hope for the best. They *react* to what a customer says, instead of effectively addressing the customer's concern. Here's one of my favorite examples:

Eric, a salesperson for X Telecommunications, meets with Lisa, general manager for a prospective client company and the final decision-maker on the new telephone system her company plans to buy. Lisa tells Eric that having a user-friendly system is an important factor in her decision.

Eric has terrific product knowledge but only rudimentary selling skills. To him, Lisa's statement is an opportunity to start talking about his product and how "user-friendly" it is. He is no longer on her agenda, but rather on his own. As a result, poor Lisa must endure listening to Eric ramble at length about his great, user-friendly telephone system.

A Superstar Sales Professional would have picked up on two key issues in Lisa's comment: *"User-friendly"* and *"Important Factor."* If Eric were a Superstar Sales Professional, he would have used two selling skills at this point to move the process forward:

- Listening skills

- Probing for clarification skills. (Finding the pain.)

He would have made Lisa feel that he was listening, and he would have encouraged her to educate him. Then he would have asked an open-ended question that invited her to tell him even more. Here are some examples:

"Lisa, you said that a user-friendly system is important. In your opinion, what would make a telephone system user-friendly?"

"Lisa, you said that a user-friendly system was important. What aspects of the system you're using now have not been user-friendly?"

"Lisa, you said that a user-friendly system was important. If there were specific functions that were at the top of your list with regard to being user-friendly, what would they be?"

Eric—the one without the selling skills—is like many of the salespeople I see and train on a regular basis. They have great product or service knowledge but weak selling skills. They have worked long and hard to be able to explain the features and the benefits of their products and services, but have spent little time mastering the skills that make a salesperson a Superstar.

How good are *your* selling skills?

Knowing that you need to effectively address objections is not enough. You must know *how* to do it. Knowing that you must negotiate price issues is not enough. You must know *how* to do it.

A couple of years ago, after completing a day of business development training with a group in Chicago, one of the attendees, "Joe," asked me if I had a few minutes to talk to him before catching a cab to the airport. I did, so we sat and talked about how the day had gone for him. He shared with me that the day's experience had been both painful and eye opening.

Joe worked for his uncle as a salesperson. He was failing miserably and feeling terrible about it. A year earlier his uncle had given him an opportunity to work for him, and Joe was humiliated that he was not producing the sales expected of him. He signed up for my class hoping it would help.

When Joe started with the company, he thought the first thing he should do was take golf lessons, because many of the salespeople in the company played golf with their customers. The company had a membership at a local country club and treated customers to lunch and rounds of golf on a regular basis.

Joe signed up for lessons, bought new clubs, and made the commitment to practice. His goal was not to become a pro but to be good enough that customers would look forward to playing golf with him. This would surely help him land some good accounts...or so he thought.

Joe's commitment to practice and develop his skills was on his mind constantly, and he played golf every free minute he could. During the winter he even went to an indoor driving range several times a week to further develop his skills. And, according to Joe, he did become a very accomplished golfer. However, after a day in my class he now understood that his selling skills were weak to non-existent.

Joe was very emotional about his struggles and said he wished he had met me a year earlier. He knew that if he had given the same dedication and commitment to developing his selling skills that he gave to improving his golf skills that he would now be an accomplished sales professional rather than just a good golfer.

I have no idea what ever happened to that young man, but I hope he is now successful. I hope he did, in fact, make the commitment to develop his selling skills with the same passion and discipline that helped him become a better golfer.

Ask yourself:

❑ What things in *my* life have taken a priority over developing my selling skills?

❑ How much time and practice have I given to becoming a Superstar Sales Professional?

❑ What have I done to make sure I am going to be successful in my chosen career?

❑ How good do I want to become and what am I willing to do to make that happen?

Key Points

➠ Before you can expect to become a Superstar Sales Professional, you must truly believe sales is an honorable and worthy profession.

➠ If you are serious about becoming a Superstar Sales Professional, you must begin with a positive mindset about your chosen career.

➠ Superstar Sales Professionals would never sell a customer a product or service that would not work for them, just to get a commission check.

➠ True salespeople honor and respect the commitments they make to their customers, to the company they represent, and to the support staff that assists them in processing the sale.

➠ Superstar Sales Professionals have discipline.

CHAPTER 2

Prospecting and Developing New Business

Whatever product or service you choose to sell, you'll find most companies expect that you find and develop your own business. Even if the company provides you with some existing customers, they want you to not only keep those customers happy, but also grow the business within those accounts—*and* go out and get new business.

So face it: Account *maintenance* is a dead position. Today, the focus is account *management*. And it can be just as challenging to keep and grow an existing account as it is to find a new one, particularly in competitive markets.

Whether you make a one-time sale or have an account that provides you with ongoing business opportunities, undying customer loyalty is no longer the norm, but rather the exception.

Is Customer Loyalty Dead?

Many people have written books on how to "partner" with customers and how to gain customer loyalty. So why do so many businesses struggle with how to keep customers for life? Why is it that even if we do a good job and offer a great product or service, we still have to "re-sell" ourselves over and over again? Why do we have to constantly look at repeat business as if it were new business and continually compete for the sale?

Before I answer that, read the following scenarios. Do any of them sound familiar?

❏   If John Smith was so happy with our product and service, why didn't he purchase his new telephone system from our company? He bought the last one from us and said he was very satisfied. We never even had a chance to submit a proposal this time!

❏   We designed their last corporate brochure and they loved it. Why did they put this one out to bid?

❏   Why do we have to respond to a request for a proposal for the new furniture for their fifth floor renovation? They've bought from us for years and we've always given them great service and quality products!

❏   How did I lose this account to a competitor when their prices are almost identical to ours? Whatever happened to customer loyalty?

Customer loyalty is still alive and well. However, *customer loyalty is no longer based on the past; it's based on the future.* Customers are more interested in how you can benefit them tomorrow than on what you did to help them yesterday. No wonder business development and account management are the keys to a salesperson's success!

Remember, the people who make buying decisions are accountable for what they do for *their* company, not for yours. They are responsible for making the right decisions for the people who sign *their* paychecks, for the bank that holds the note, or for the stockholders who want a return on their investments.

While they may like you and trust you and may even want to give you their business, they are also held to a higher standard than in the past. The purchasing decisions they make will ultimately reflect, positively or negatively, on them, not you. As such, they are more cautious, do more comparing, and research prices more than ever before. Why? Well, it's just *so easy* to do.

Think about it: Time and technology have transformed the way we do business. People are busy, and the Internet has simplified how customers and prospects research products, services, price, and even reputation. To those of us who sell, the Internet is a friend one day and an enemy the next.

Active existing accounts, previous customers, and new prospects all have one thing in mind when deciding who gets their business: *"What's in this for me?*" As such, we need to treat every sales opportunity as a first time sale and be ready to prove ourselves once more. We can never take "partnering" for granted or assume the sale will just happen. Gaining repeat business is a privilege we earn over and over again, not a binding contract.

Superstar Prospecting

Superstar Sales Professionals know that business will not simply come to them. They recognize the need to go after it. They don't sit around waiting for the phone to ring, an e-mail to pop up on the computer, or an envelope to arrive in the mail awarding them business. Superstar Sales Professionals are proactive rather than reactive. They look for opportunity; they do not wait for it.

A client once told me, "I have enough salespeople waiting for the wave and even more riding the wave. I want the ones who can create the wave." I'm not sure where he came up with that analogy, but it's a good one.

Superstar Sales Professionals *never* stop looking for business. They never assume they will get the next sale based on the last one. They are actively seeking every opportunity, within existing accounts and with prospects, to offer new value and position their product or service as *the* solution for the customer's needs.

To become the Superstar Sales Professional who *creates the wave*, you must believe that prospecting is not illegal, indecent, or immoral. Prospecting is simply the way you get new business.

When you pick up the phone or drop in unannounced to make a cold call or a warm call where you may have some advance information, always ask yourself three questions:

- Am I bothering this person?

- Would the prospect prefer that I went away?

- Will he or she view me as an interruption?

Most of the time, the answer to all three questions is "yes." Yes, we are a bother. Yes, the prospect often wishes we would go away. And, yes, the person generally views us as an interruption. Welcome to the world of prospecting! What did you *think* it was all about? If you can't become comfortable with having to make contact with someone who might not be thrilled to hear from you, you may want to consider another career.

When it comes to prospecting, we have two responsibilities as sales professionals: 1) Make contact with people who are, ***initially***, not interested in hearing about what we have to offer, and 2) Get them interested and wanting to find out more.

That's called *selling*!

When salespeople tell me—and they often do—that they don't like prospecting because they feel like they are bothering people, I tell them they should consider a different career. And, yes, business-to-business selling is a career, not a job.

If your company provides you with leads where prospects welcome your call or visit, then someone else has done the initial prospecting and your job is to win the business. Realize, however, that such a scenario is the exception rather than the norm.

Why would companies *not* have someone do the initial prospecting and appointment setting for their salespeople? Because it's an expensive way to do business, and it has a very low return on investment.

In addition, the skills necessary to do an effective job of prospecting and appointment setting are not much different from what's needed to go in and get the business. Those who prospect must be persistent and inquisitive, as well as good listeners and articulate communicators. They must also be able to effectively address objections and ask for the appointment.

As such, people who are effective at finding and qualifying opportunities, and then getting the door open for a salesperson, are not working for an hourly wage and a spiff per appointment set. Today, good business development reps often make as much as good salespeople. The era of "Tillie Telemarketer," smiling and dialing to set appointments for salespeople, is over.

Prospecting today is not just about numbers; it's about opportunity and timing. Salespeople want *qualified* appointments. Meeting with people because they are breathing and have a pulse is too often a waste of time. Anyone in sales knows there is a big difference between a suspect and a qualified prospect. Focusing *only* on getting an appointment and then *hoping* it turns out to be a qualified opportunity can be time consuming, expensive, and risky.

Before you meet with any prospect, whether it's an appointment you set yourself or one someone else set for you, know the answers to the following two questions:

❑ **Am I meeting with the true decision-maker?**

Why would you want to meet with someone who can't say "yes"? And if that person rejects doing business with you and you go over his or her head, you might create an enemy inside the company who will work against you. Even if that person says "yes," you still have to *hope* he or she can convince the true decision-maker to move forward. Unless this person is willing to let you meet with the true decision-maker—and that's often not the case—you are now dependent on someone else's ability to influence the sale, which can be very risky.

Meeting with the wrong person is not the way to be successful in sales. Therefore, always remember the following phrase: ***"Never take no from a person who can't say yes."*** I don't know where or when I first heard that, but it has stuck with me for many years. It's one of the best things I learned early in my sales career.

❑ **Is there potential for business?**

The last thing you want to do is meet with a decision-maker only to find out the chances for you to do business together are slim to none. In this scenario, you get quality time with the prospect, and he or she gets quality information from you, only to find out the person has little need for what you have to offer, would never spend the money to buy it, wants to place an order that is so small and hardly worth your time and effort, or has a brother-in-law in the business and can get the same thing at cost.

Appointment setting only for the purpose of appointment setting is costly. Nothing comes from nothing, and Superstar Sales Professionals put a high value on their time and energy. They want qualified appointments rather than a large number of unqualified appointments.

Do Today's Companies Want YOU?

Because "getting in" is one of the most important and difficult steps in the sales process, more and more companies want salespeople who can do it all. They want the Superstar Sales Professional who can find it, qualify it, develop it, close it, grow it, and keep it.

Today's sales professionals must make sure their prospecting skills are as good as their product knowledge and their ability to close sales. How do you get to that point? We'll find out in our next chapter.

Key Points

- ➠ Account *maintenance* is a dead position. Today's focus is account *management*.

- ➠ Customer loyalty is no longer based on the past; it's based on the future.

- ➠ People who make buying decisions are accountable for what they do for *their* company, not for yours.

- ➠ Time and technology have transformed the way we do business.

- ➠ Superstar Sales Professionals know that business will not simply come to them. They recognize the need to go after it.

- ➠ When prospecting, we need to accept that our call is not always going to be welcomed.

- ➠ Prospecting today is not just about numbers; it's about opportunity and timing.

- ➠ Salespeople want *qualified* appointments, not just appointments.

- ➠ Make sure you are meeting with the *true* decision maker. Never accept "No" from a person who can't say "Yes."

CHAPTER 3

Preparation and Attitude

How often can we just walk into a company and expect that the decision-maker will stop what he or she is doing and meet with us? And what if the decision maker does agree to meet with us, but after an hour or so with the person, we determine there is no potential for business?

Is either of these scenarios the ideal way of going after business? No!

For years, I've encouraged salespeople to stop that kind of prospecting. I've told sales managers that cold calling door-to-door is no longer the most effective way to meet and greet prospective customers.

Kicking your salespeople out of the office at 8:30 in the morning because you believe they should be out there banging on doors accomplishes only one thing: It drives them to the nearest coffee house for a café latte with all the other salespeople who were kicked out of their offices at 8:30 that same morning.

While cold calling door-to-door has been challenging for years, it's become even more difficult after the events of 9-11, particularly when calling on large corporations. Today, you're naïve to think you'll be able to talk to anyone, other than a security guard, without an appointment.

Even when you can get in, asking to see the person who makes decisions about your products or services sends a message that you believe whatever that person is doing can be easily interrupted. Just asking to see them can often burn bridges, particularly if the company has "No Soliciting" signs on the doors.

Playing the numbers game door-to-door can be one of the biggest time wasters for salespeople today. While some people *will* see you, how many of them turn out to be qualified prospects? Unfortunately, far too few. Even worse, what happens to the ones who refuse to see you when you just drop in? What alternate plan do you have to get *their* business?

As you can tell, I place very little value on cold calling door-to-door as the primary way to meet with decision-makers and find business. Quite simply, it's a huge waste of time. However, the word *"stupid"* is not written on my forehead.

I've told salespeople for years that I can work an office complex, a building, or a downtown area like a mouse looking for a new hoard of food. However, when I do that, my objective is not necessarily to meet with decision-makers at that time; rather, my goal is to gather enough quality information to determine whom to contact for an appointment, and if this is an opportunity I want to pursue.

The ability to gain quality information when prospecting face-to-face or by telephone is often what separates sales "wannabe's" from Superstar Sales Professionals.

Let's talk first about techniques for gaining that information by telephone, and then later, I'll address how to do that when cold calling in person.

The Telephone Is Not A Tool To Make An Appointment ... It *IS* An Appointment!

That's a reality. Business people no longer call other business people just to schedule an appointment to talk or meet. The call itself is often "the appointment." The need to meet face-to-face is no longer critical to conducting business.

Today, many people discuss, plan, modify, and negotiate business via phone. And while we may eventually need to meet face-to-face to sell our particular product or service, we can exchange much information by telephone in advance. As such, telephone prospecting has become the norm, not the exception. Today it represents one of the most effective ways for business-to-business salespeople to find qualified leads.

Q: What are the keys to successful telephone prospecting?

A: Preparation, Attitude, and Skill.

Preparation Makes Perfect

Schedule time for prospecting and never give it up unless you have no choice. I know people who schedule time for prospecting and then pray for something to come up that will provide them with an excuse to cancel it. They allow themselves to get caught up in non-revenue producing tasks and then claim it's not their fault they lack time to prospect.

When salespeople tell me they do not have enough time to prospect, I generally ask them, "What does your W2 read? How much money are you making?" I tell them not to answer out loud but to get that figure in their head.

If you are not earning what you should or could be earning, then you might need to change how you are using your time. In sales there is a big difference between *activity* and *productivity*. Many of you have heard that before, but do you *really* understand what it means?

For example, if you find yourself doing mundane clerical and administrative tasks, checking e-mails, or returning non-time sensitive voice mails during peak selling hours, you're doing task activities and likely won't have time to prospect for new business. Ultimately, that will reflect on your sales numbers.

I've met many sales professionals who would do practically anything to avoid rescheduling a dental or hair appointment. Heaven forbid we would not get our teeth cleaned or our hair styled on a timely basis. Yet those same people will give up time previously allocated for prospecting without even thinking about it, even though the prospecting often provides the income necessary to pay the dentist and the hair stylist!

Schedule time for prospecting on your appointment calendar and treat that time with the same sanctity and dedication you give an appointment with an existing customer, your hair stylist, or your dentist.

Allocate dedicated time blocks—between ninety minutes and two hours—for each prospecting session, and stay on schedule. Prospecting takes time and energy. You must keep at it long enough to produce results and get the momentum going. If you haven't yet had the experience of "getting on a roll," you're missing out on one of the most exciting "rushes" true sales professionals experience.

It's not enough to take twenty minutes to make a few calls before leaving the office for an appointment or going to lunch. Striking gold after panning for fifteen to twenty minutes may make good storybook material, but in the real world, it rarely happens that way.

Committing a block of time to telephone prospecting means just that. During this time, you do not check or return e-mails or voice mail. You do not take incoming calls, get involved in conversations with others in the office, write letters, prepare quotes, get coffee, or go to the bathroom. You do all those "activities" either before or after your prospecting. Superstar Sales Professionals take their prospecting time seriously and they protect it. They know it is critical to their continued success.

How many prospecting sessions should you schedule per month? Again, look at your W2. If you are making the kind of money you want to be making, then you may only need to schedule an occasional block of time for prospecting.

However, if you are struggling or are new to sales and attempting to build your book of business, then you likely need several blocks a week of telephone prospecting time until you are up and running. Prospecting is something you should never stop. It's not just for keeping the funnel full. It's for keeping the funnel from becoming empty.

Let me share what happened with one of my client's reps. In the interest of protecting her privacy, we'll call her Lisa.

Lisa is a seasoned salesperson with five years' experience selling advertising for a well-known magazine. She consistently made quota but was frustrated because her income stayed about the same every year.

While talking with her, we determined she spent far too much unnecessary time on existing accounts and not enough time on finding new ones. And the reason was nothing more than her comfort level. She simply avoided prospecting because she could.

She had gotten into the habit of doing too much "busy work" during peak selling times, and she had enough business to make that easy to do. However, this bad habit was costing her money, and she wanted that to change.

First, we looked at her weekly planner and isolated two, two-hour blocks of time per week for four straight weeks for telephone prospecting. Lisa made the commitment to stick to her prospecting schedule, no matter what. If one of her clients wanted to meet with her, she would avoid setting appointments that might conflict with any of her prospecting time slots.

The plan worked, and Lisa found some great leads that ultimately turned into accounts. In just nine months, her income increased by over $18,000.

I further helped by coaching her on prospecting skills and making sure she was confident and competent for the task at hand. However, she would not have attained success if she had not been willing to allocate the time and stick to the plan.

Another key to successful telephone prospecting is making sure you have your list of contacts prepared in advance. Do whatever you must to ensure enough quality time for advance preparations. Come in early, stay late, or skip lunch, but know who you are planning to call *before* you sit down to make the calls.

Unless you prepare in advance, your prospecting will be like shopping at a large mall for holiday gifts for friends and family, and you have no idea of what they want or need. You'll quickly become stressed, waste time, and eventually give up. In sales, trying to figure out *whom* to call can be as trying as the call itself and a big time waster, so plan ahead to avoid disaster.

The complexity of your product or service and market potential usually determines the number of contacts you will initially need on your calling list. For most people, somewhere between thirty-five and fifty names is usually a good number to start with for a two-hour session. We all know we're going to be confronted with a lot of voice mail and skilled gatekeepers—that's just the way it is. As such, make sure you have enough contacts to last the entire session.

Keep in mind that unless you are a rookie and just starting out, not all of your calls will necessarily be cold calls. Some might be follow-up calls, referrals from other customers, people requesting information, and even inactive accounts.

Utilizing a good contact management program is also important. Many programs are available today, and most are relatively inexpensive. Contact management enables you to document what happens when you make contact with a prospective customer, and ensures you don't miss the appropriate next step. A good contact management program can also be a great help in building rapport. Here is an example:

You noted in your contact management file that you spoke with Joe, a key decision-maker and a qualified prospect, on March 18. At that time he was not open to meeting with you because his company was in the midst of switching to a new computer system, and he was bogged down with problems. You agreed to call him back in a couple of weeks when things might be running smoother. You scheduled the call back date in your contact management program and you probably won't think about that prospect again until that time.

Two weeks later, when it's time to call Joe back, your contact management program alerts you of the necessary callback. You look at your prior notes and recall the conversation about his problems with the new computer system. Now, you have a great way to immediately create some dialog:

> *"Joe, the last time we talked you were knee-deep in computer problems. How are things going for you now?"*

Joe may or may not want to talk about his computer problems, but it will be obvious to him that you listened the last time you talked. And that can be an important step to building trust and rapport.

Contact management is a tool that helps Superstar Sales Professionals be successful. They would never think about prospecting without a way to document what happened and a system that ensures they do any and all necessary follow-up on a timely basis.

Q: What is the worst time to schedule cold calls?

A: Monday morning.

What are you like on Monday morning? Statistics indicate most business decision-makers are least receptive to receiving unsolicited sales calls on Monday morning. Even if you run across a few who don't mind, why play the odds?

Q: What are the best times to schedule cold calls?

A: Actually, any time other than Monday morning.

Some will argue that Friday afternoon is a total loss because decision-makers and business owners often knock off early. I disagree. I've found Fridays can be very productive. While I agree you may find fewer decision-makers available, the ones you reach are often mellow, relaxed, and looking forward to the weekend. Next week's schedule of things to do seems light years away. Don't discount the value of making prospecting calls on Friday afternoon.

One last point when it comes to preparation: Prospect when you are at your best and when you are at your highest energy level, not when you are in "low gear."

For example, I'm a morning person. My feet hit the floor at 5:30-6:00 a.m., and I'm a ball of energy. At about 3.00 p.m., my energy starts to drain. I know that about myself and use that knowledge when scheduling my "to do" lists.

When are *you* at your best? Make sure you know and take that into consideration when allocating time for prospecting.

Now let's move on to the second key to successful telephone prospecting: **Attitude**.

When salespeople need to prospect, they typically resist, procrastinate, and don't prepare. Why is that?

Attitude, Attitude, Attitude!

Attitude is Everything

Remember the guy in the blue polyester suit that was three sizes too small for him? That's how many salespeople view people who prospect. They feel they are doing something Mother would not approve of, and that there has to be a better way to be successful.

They sit at their desks and pray, "Dear God, please let the phone ring and let it be a new customer who wants to buy something right now." And they'd give almost anything if their sales manager would walk up and hand them ten hot prospects who want a salesperson to call them right away. Don't we wish it were that easy?

In Chapter Two I said that prospecting was not illegal, indecent, or immoral but rather the way you do business.

Consider the facts:

❑   If you can't buy into the fact that you must prospect and are overly concerned that you might be bothering someone or doing something you should not be doing, you will never be a Superstar Sales Professional.

❑   If you are overly concerned with pleasing or accommodating others and you view prospecting as pushy and offensive, you will never be a Superstar Sales Professional.

❑   If you convince yourself before you even make the first call that your prospects will not be interested, have no money, or are too happy with their current vendor to listen to you, you will never be a Superstar Sales Professional.

❑ If you believe you can send enough information by mail or e-mail so that prospects will eventually call you instead of you having to cold call them, you will never be a Superstar Sales Professional.

❑ If you believe your company is responsible for providing you with enough hot leads and confirmed qualified appointments to make a good living, you will never be a Superstar Sales Professional.

If any of these statements describe what you think about prospecting, you will never be a Superstar Sales Professional . . . until you change your attitude.

I once read that attitudes are outer reflections of inner feelings. That statement could not be truer when it comes to sales. So many things that salespeople do well or do not do well relate to how they *feel* about what they are doing. If you have a negative attitude about prospecting, then you will never do it well.

Let me give my thirty-second "Winnie tells it the way it is" speech:

If you are in sales for any reason other than to win and to make money, then do everybody a favor and get out. Sales is about money. It's about selling a product or service that creates a profit for your company and an income for you and others.

If you want a career in sales because you "like people," let me suggest a career with the Red Cross or a similar non-profit organization.

Just for a moment, think about all the people who work for your company who are not in sales. They answer the phones, provide customer support, drive the trucks, pack the boxes, do the payroll, manage employee benefits, keep the computers working, and clean the office, just for starters.

Their job security depends heavily on how well the salespeople perform. When sales are flat, companies lay off people, cut benefits, freeze salaries, and some even fold. When salespeople are not performing at an acceptable level, they put everyone at risk. That's why the ability to prospect successfully is so important. Sales drives the entire organization.

"Effective Salespeople Are Essential . . . Not Optional!"

My clients have heard me say that over and over, and that quote is even printed on the cover of my workbooks. I reinforce that thought in all my sales training classes.

Now that you've eliminated any negative thoughts about prospecting and concerns about becoming like the man in the blue polyester suit, we're ready to address the third key to successful telephone prospecting—**Skill**, which we'll address in our next chapter.

Key Points

➠ **The Telephone Is Not A Tool To Make An Appointment ... It _IS_ An Appointment!**

➠ The keys to successful telephone prospecting are Preparation, Attitude, and Skill.

➠ Allocate time on a regular basis for prospecting and never give up that time unless it's truly unavoidable.

➠ Allocate at least ninety minutes to two hours per prospecting session so you can build momentum and increase your opportunity for success.

➠ Monday morning is the worst time to make cold calls.

➠ Prospect when you are at your highest energy level.

➠ Schedule prospecting sessions as often as needed to ensure your W2 is where it should be.

➠ Come in early, stay late, or skip lunch, but make sure you have your calling list ready before you sit down to make your calls (thirty-five to fifty names are generally enough for a two-hour session).

➠ Use a contact management program to document how the call went and schedule the next appropriate step for follow-up.

➠ Prospecting is not illegal, indecent, or immoral. It's the way business is done.

"Effective Salespeople are Essential. . .Not Optional!"

CHAPTER 4

Prospecting Skills

Superstar Sales Professionals possess five key prospecting skills:

- They have the ability to identify the true decision-maker.

- They have the ability to make contact with the decision-maker and gain his or her attention.

- They have the ability to confidently ask for the business.

- They have the ability to effectively address the first objection or resistance to the call.

- They have the ability to position themselves for the future when now is not an option.

Skill #1: The Ability to Identify the True Decision-Maker.

If you're lucky, you will know who the decision-maker is prior to making a prospecting call. However, many sales professionals don't. And those situations call for specific techniques you can use to obtain the vital information you need.

First, let's recognize what we're up against. Most receptionists, secretaries, customer support staff, etc. have received specific instructions on how to respond when salespeople call seeking information or asking to speak to someone. The typical protocol is:

- ❑ Do not give out any information.

- ❑ Do not put the call through to the person the salesperson is attempting to reach.

- ❑ Tell the salesperson to mail information; if we're interested, we'll call them.

Who can blame companies for taking that attitude? Some business professionals receive so many calls from salespeople that if they were to talk them all, they would never get any of their own work done.

And if they do take a call and find time for a meeting, all too often they find themselves listening to an ill-prepared salesperson who talks non-stop and is totally focused on his or her own agenda.

We're going to take an entirely different approach.

First, let's look at a typical telephone prospecting call:

Receptionist: "Good morning, Jones Advertising Agency. This is Jill."

Salesperson: "Hi Jill. This is Don Williams with Contract Printers. I'd like to talk to the person who takes care of your company's printing needs. Would he or she be available?"

Receptionist: "And the purpose of your call?"

Salesperson: "I just wanted to see if I could talk to them about what kind of printing needs your company has and see if we could present a quote for your business."

Receptionist: "Just a moment and I'll see if he's available."

(Our caller is then placed on hold for two minutes listening to elevator music.)

Receptionist: "Sir, our marketing department said to tell you they are not interested in changing printers at this time, but if you would like to send some information they would be happy to keep it on file."

Salesperson: "Okay, who would I send that to?"

Receptionist: "Just send it to the attention of Marketing. Our address is 1301 East Jefferson Avenue."

How typical was that sales call? And how much did the salesperson accomplish?

Salespeople often use language that sabotages their prospecting success. And mistake Number One is asking to *speak* to or asking for *the name of* the person they need to contact.

When that happens, the gatekeepers kick into gear and block the call. You'll hear things like:

❑ May I tell him who's calling?

❑ Is she expecting your call?

❑ And the purpose of your call?

❑ What is this regarding?

❑ I'm sorry; I'm not permitted to give out that information.

If you've been in sales for more than a month you've probably heard all of the above and more.

The next most common mistake salespeople make is how they describe who they want to contact:

❑ The person who takes care of widgets.

❑ The person in charge of buying widgets.

❑ The person who purchases the widgets.

❑ The person who orders your widgets.

❑ The person who handles widgets.

❑ The person responsible for your widgets.

Note that none of those terms mentions anything about the person *who makes decisions* about anything.

Superstar Sales Professionals know the importance of meeting with and talking with true decision-makers. So at this point, uncovering that detail is key to their success.

Unskilled prospectors too often end up talking to someone who may process an order, gather information about an order, or even assist in the selection. But if that person does not have the authority to make a final decision, your search for new business may already be in trouble.

Granted, you will sometimes find yourself in situations where you have no choice but to work with someone other than the decision-maker. But Superstar Sales Professionals will do everything they can—and they have practiced their techniques long and hard—to prevent that from happening.

Ask yourself: "Do I find myself talking with or meeting with the wrong person many times, or does it happen only occasionally?"

If you frequently lose selling opportunities because you communicate with someone who has no authority to sign the check, then you must do something about it!

So how can we prevent being screened out and improve our chances of getting to the right person? Well, let's listen to sales professional Don Williams with Contract Printers as he tries a *new* approach to making a prospecting call.

> *Receptionist: "Good morning, Jones Advertising Agency. This is Jill."*

> *Salesperson: "Hello Jill, this is Don Williams with Contract Printers. I have some information I'd like to forward to the person who makes the decisions about your company's printing needs. Who should I send this to?"*

> *Receptionist: "That would probably be Denise Long."*

> *Salesperson: "Great. And for my records, what is her position?"*

> *Receptionist: "Denise is in charge of advertising and marketing."*

> *Salesperson: "Thank you, you've been very helpful. By chance, would Denise be available to speak with me?"*

For now, let's not think about the response to our request to speak with Denise. Instead, let's look at what we've accomplished up to this point.

At the very least we now have a name and a position. And knowing the person's position often validates that the name the gatekeeper gave us is the right one.

Quick Tip: You will get more information if you use the term "position" as opposed to "title." Many times, the receptionist won't know everyone's exact title. On the other hand, he or she will most likely know what a person does or that person's department responsibilities.

What was different about our new approach? Why was the receptionist so willing to give us the decision-maker's name and position?

First, we made reference to sending information rather than immediately asking to speak to someone or asking for the person's name without giving a reason for asking. We simply said, *"I'd like to forward information to the person who makes the decisions about _____. Who should I send this to?"*

We use the term "send information" with one objective only: To help us gain the name of the person we ultimately wish to contact. By doing so, you appear much less threatening to the person answering the phone, and he or she may even think the information was requested. However, resist sending anything in the mail or even by e-mail until you have talked to your prospect and decided that sending something would be mutually beneficial.

Businesses get a small mountain of brochures, catalogs and samples every day, and most of them end up in the same place—the wastebasket. So I'm not suggesting you get the decision-maker's name and the position and then run immediately to the mailroom to send out a sales or marketing packet. Most likely, your information would also end up in the wastebasket. Remember, we're attempting to gain the decision-maker's name so we can eventually make contact with him or her.

Now let's address the second big difference: Our use of the term "makes the decisions."

Our salesperson said, *"I have some information I'd like to forward to the person who makes the decisions."* This is far more effective than asking for the person "who takes care of ..." or "who does the buying for ..." or "who is responsible for ..." We want the order *maker*, not the order *placer*.

In some cases, the person answering the telephone may have no idea who the key decision-maker might be. On the other hand, when you say, "makes the decisions," you have a much better chance of at least getting someone at a management level, rather than someone in a clerical, administrative, or support position.

Always aim to speak with someone as high up in the organization as possible. Working down is much easier than trying to go up the corporate ladder.

Here are some other ways to say the same thing:

> *"Person who makes the decisions regarding ..."*
>
> *"Person who decides where you purchase ..."*
>
> *"Individual responsible for decisions concerning ..."*

Once we have determined the decision-maker's name and position we can then attempt to get that person on the telephone.

> *"By chance would she be available to speak with me?"*
>
> *"Is it possible to speak to her for a few minutes?"*
>
> *"Is she available at this time?"*

While actually getting through on the first attempt would be a nice bonus, at this point it's not critical. The key thing is that you now have the decision maker's name and position and can try to reach that person later.

Sound Successful

Successful prospecting in this manner calls for another key ingredient: Attitude. Superstar Sales Professionals do not apologize for calling and they do not sound like they are doing something that borders on illegal, indecent, or immoral. When making prospecting calls you must sound:

- Confident

- Professional

- Important

Here is a great way to make sure you do: Tape-record your prospecting calls, even if you just tape your end of the conversation. After listening to the tape, ask yourself, "Did I sound confident, professional, and important, or did I sound like I was doing something I should not be doing and would give anything to get out of doing?"

In sales, attitude plays a big part in determining how successful you'll be. You must believe that you are one businessperson attempting to reach another businessperson and that it's okay to do so. There is nothing dirty, sleazy, or immoral about making a prospecting call when you have a legitimate product or service to offer.

Hearing how you sound when making your prospecting calls can be a tremendous help in perfecting your selling skills. Why? Because we rarely hear ourselves the way we really talk; rather, we hear ourselves the way we *think* we talk. Using a tape recorder makes everything clear and tells us where we need to practice for improvement.

I'll mention the use of the tape recorder frequently in this book; so if you do not own one now, buy one. I promise it will be the best tool you can have to help develop and perfect your selling skills.

Let's look at another call using the same techniques we've been discussing:

Receptionist: "Good afternoon, Evergreen Law Offices."

Salesperson: "Good afternoon, this is Sandy Whitt with Central Business Interiors. I'm attempting to send some information to the person who will be making office furniture decisions for your new building. Who should I forward this to?"

Receptionist: "Jason Edwards."

Salesperson: "Okay. And what is his position with the company?"

Receptionist: "Jason is Vice President of Finance."

Salesperson: "Thank you. Is he available to speak with me at this time?"

Now we all know that the chances our salesperson will reach the decision-maker on the first attempt are slim. Once in a while we'll get lucky, but if it were that easy I would not have written this book and you would not be reading it!

Most likely we'll hear something like:

> *Receptionist: "He's not in the office. Would you like his voice mail?"*

At this point, far too many salespeople simply opt to leave a voice mail message asking the decision-maker to return his or her call. And we all know the odds of *that* happening.

Leave a voice mail message when prospecting and you run the risk of losing too much control of the situation. The decision-maker now knows who you are and why you are calling and may avoid your calls even more. Prospecting is somewhat like playing poker—you don't want to show your hand too soon.

Q: So what should you do when you constantly have to deal with voice mail?

A: Do what the Superstar Sales Professionals do and don't be so quick to leave a message. Instead, try to get more information. Here's one way to do that:

> *Receptionist: "Good afternoon, Evergreen Law Offices."*
>
> *Salesperson: "Good afternoon, this is Sandy Whitt with Central Business Interiors. I'm attempting to send some information to the person who will be making office furniture decisions for your new building. Who should I forward this to?"*
>
> *Receptionist: "Jason Edwards."*
>
> *Salesperson: "Okay. And what is his position?"*
>
> *Receptionist: "Jason is Vice President of Finance."*
>
> *Salesperson: "Thank you. Is he available to speak with me at this time?"*
>
> *Receptionist: "He's not in the office today. Would you like his voice mail?"*
>
> *Salesperson: "No thanks. I'm going to be in and out a lot myself*

and I don't want to cause telephone tag. What's his extension and I'll try him later in the week?"

Receptionist: "Jason's extension is 876."

Salesperson: "Thanks for your help."

One important tip about asking for the extension: Be direct; don't be wishy-washy. Assume your decision-maker has an extension and ask for it. *"What's his extension and I'll try him later?*

Never say:

"Would you happen to know his extension?"

"Would it be possible to get his extension?"

"Do you think I could have his extension?"

Superstar Sales Professionals would ask: "What is his extension and I'll try him later?"

What does our salesperson have now? She has the name and position of the decision-maker and his extension. As such, her next attempt to reach Jason might sound like this:

Receptionist: "Good afternoon, Evergreen Law Offices."

Salesperson: "Good afternoon, extension 876 please."

And that is all that's necessary. While it sounds simple, far too many salespeople go overboard. Here are some examples of what we ***don't*** want to say.

Receptionist: "Good morning, Jones Advertising Agency. This is Jill."

Salesperson: "Good morning. My name is Don Williams with Contract Printers. Would it be possible to speak to Denise Long?"

Or,

Receptionist: "Good afternoon, Evergreen Law Firm."

Salesperson: "Hi, this is Sandy with Central Business Interiors. Could I talk to Jason Edwards at extension 876 please?"

The more you talk, the more chance you have of being screened. Ask only for the extension and you will have a far better chance of just being transferred.

Salesperson: "Good afternoon, extension 876 please."

While this will not guarantee you'll make contact with your decision-maker, it will give you a much better chance of getting to the telephone that sits on your decision-maker's desk.

If you get voice mail when you call your prospect, simply hang up without leaving a message. You may have to do that several times before actually connecting.

Q: What if the decision-maker has caller ID and knows you have called several times without leaving a message?

A: If that ever comes up, you simply explain you are out of the office or on the telephone a lot yourself. You did not want to leave a message when you were not sure you would be available to take his or her return call.

The desire to avoid creating telephone tag is a very legitimate and professional reason for not leaving a voice mail message. However, our main reason for not leaving messages when prospecting by telephone is that we suspect our prospect probably will not return our call anyway.

Let's look at all this again, only this time, read aloud and play both the role of the receptionist and your own role as a sales professional. Repeat it several times until you feel comfortable and confident. Get out the tape recorder, record the exercise, and play it back.

Ask yourself if you sounded Confident, Professional, and Important. Keep practicing and reviewing until you are comfortable using *your* choice of words without changing the technique. Practice makes Superstar Sales Professionals.

Receptionist: "Good afternoon, Evergreen Law Offices."

Salesperson: "Good afternoon, this is Sandy Whitt with Central Business Interiors. I'm attempting to send some information to the person who will be making office furniture decisions for your new building. Who should I forward this to?"

↳ *suppose they don't know?*

Receptionist: "Jason Edwards."

Salesperson: "Thank you. And for my records, what is Jason's position with the company?"

Receptionist: "Jason is Vice President of Finance."

Salesperson: "Would he be available to speak with me at this time?"

Receptionist: "He's not in the office. Would you like his voice mail"

Salesperson: "No thanks, I'm going to be in and out a lot myself and I don't want to cause telephone tag. What's his extension and I'll try him later in the week?"

Receptionist: "Jason's extension is 876."

Salesperson: "Thanks for your help."

Q: What happens if I do everything right and I've tried several times and still can't get my decision-maker on the telephone?

A: Keep trying!

Try calling a few minutes before the company switchboard opens in the morning or a few minutes after it closes at the end of the day. You would be surprised how often this can result in an opportunity to talk to the person you have been trying to reach. When the telephone on their desk rings, most people will not let it go unanswered just because no one is there to screen the call.

Another option is to call on a Saturday morning. If you are serious about your product or service and you know you must reach the right person, why *not* Saturday morning? People with positions of responsibility often work long hours and Saturday morning is no exception. Be polite, and if it's not a good time to talk, attempt to schedule a better time.

Calling once and leaving a message will rarely work. Superstar Sales Professionals have "stick-to-itiveness." They stay the course until they have tried numerous times to reach their presumed decision-maker. And if that does not work, they try something different. Be persistent and tenacious.

Let's look at some of your options for trying something different.

- Leave a voice mail message.

- Send an e-mail.

- Ask to speak to your decision-maker's assistant or secretary and see if you can learn something that will help you get a foot in the door.

- Send a (brief) letter along with some company information.

- Review your prospect's web site for information that could assist you in getting to someone with clout or influence.

- Determine if you know someone who might be able to get you an introduction.

- Begin your "Touching Program." (We'll talk more about this later.)

- Do all of the above and more.

However, nothing is as effective as an actual conversation by telephone or face-to-face. No one can sell *you* better than *you*. As such, implement Plan B *only* when you know you have done everything you can to make verbal contact with your decision-maker by telephone or in person.

In my years in sales management and as a consultant I have seen hundreds of sales call reports that read as follows:

"Left message but they did not return my call."

If you are among the many salespeople filing that kind of sales report, let me ask you two questions:

❑   What effort have you put forth that an untrained high school student could not have done?

❑   What are you doing to demonstrate you are a professional salesperson who understands that being persistent and tenacious is how Superstar Sales Professionals set themselves apart from the wannabes?

Cold Calling in Person

I mentioned earlier that I would address face-to-face prospecting. While there is nothing wrong with walking through a building or an office complex seeking information, your sole purpose should not be to immediately meet with key decision-makers.

I have a sign on my office door that says, "We see sales professionals by appointment only." If salespeople violate that rule they burn a bridge with me—one they *can't* repair. They have chosen to assume that my work is not really important, and that they can easily interrupt me.

On the other hand, why not use the same technique you would use on the telephone when you make a face-to-face sales call? It's less intrusive and far more professional. Here is an example of what I mean:

> *Receptionist: "May I help you?"*
>
> *Salesperson: "Yes. I was in the area calling on a customer and wanted to stop in and get some information. My name is Jim Lucas and I work for Dalton's Computer Services. I'd like to send some information about our services to the person in your company who makes the decisions regarding computer equipment and software needs. Who would you suggest I send that to?"*
>
> *Receptionist: "You can send that to Eric Steiner."*
>
> *Salesperson: "And what is his position with your company?"*
>
> *Receptionist: "He's the owner."*
>
> *Salesperson: "Thanks so much for your help. You've been great. May I ask, does he ever see salespeople without an appointment?"*

Receptionist: "No, he doesn't. You would have to call and arrange that with his secretary."

Salesperson: "Well, thanks for your honesty and your help. One last question, what are the chances I could have one of his business cards?"

Receptionist: "Just a minute and I'll get one for you."

No bridges burned. No unhappy executive because a salesperson is trying to barge in when he or she is busy. In addition, our salesperson was able to get the name and position of the decision-maker *and* a business card, which usually provides an e-mail address and extension.

Occasionally, you may find the receptionist very open, chatty, and willing to talk to you. When that happens you might even find out who the decision-maker buys from, what he or she buys, and how often.

Any information you can get helps in making sure you are tracking down the right person and determining what you need to do to meet with that individual.

In some cases, you'll even learn enough to indicate this is not a good prospect. Now you can move on and not waste your time.

Most receptionists know if the person you are attempting to meet will see salespeople without an appointment. Trust the gatekeeper's judgment, get as much information as you can, and do not push the issue of seeing them at that time.

Superstar Sales Professionals do not push or pull. They are persistent and tenacious investigators. They know they have a myriad of ways to accomplish their prospecting objectives, and they use them all.

Banging on doors and asking to see key decision-makers is an outdated and unacceptable approach to prospecting. It is, however, a great way to gain quality information about the person who will be making the decisions regarding the products or services you have to offer.

One last thing to remember when prospecting door-to-door: Do not carry the information you mentioned sending to the decision-maker in your hands. Keep it in your briefcase so that when the receptionist suggests you just "leave it with her," you can say you do not have it with you.

Leaving your materials with the receptionist can tip your hand too soon with the prospect. Even worse, the receptionist could pitch your materials in the wastebasket, assuming the decision-maker will not be interested.

We've addressed the importance of being persistent and tenacious when prospecting. On the other hand, even Superstar Sales Professionals will, on occasion, have to resort to Plan B—The Touching Program—because they have been unable to make verbal contact with the decision-maker. We'll address that later in this book. For now, let's move to our next chapter, which addresses what to do when we finally connect with the person we believe has the decision-making authority.

Key Points

➨ Making reference to "sending information" is less threatening to the receptionist and you will have a much better chance of getting the decision-maker's name.

➨ Using the phrase "makes the decisions" is more effective than "takes care of," "in charge of," or "does the purchasing of." "Makes the decisions" will get you to the management level more often.

➨ Once you have a name, ask for the position. *"And his position, please?"* This helps validate you are attempting to reach the right person.

➨ Once you have the name and position, by all means ask to speak with the person, but do it almost as an afterthought. *"By chance, would she be available to talk to me?"*

➨ Don't be too quick to leave messages asking for your call to be returned when the decision-maker doesn't know who you are or what you want. Don't show your hand too soon.

➨ Get the decision-maker's extension. This helps you get to the telephone on the decision-maker's desk and reduces call screening.

➨ When making prospecting calls by telephone you must sound Confident, Professional, and Important.

➨ When making face-to-face prospecting calls, do not carry materials in your hand. Keep them in your briefcase.

➠ Use a tape recorder to practice and perfect what you are going to say when making prospecting calls.

➠ Try calling a few minutes before the switchboard opens or after it closes if you are having trouble connecting with the decision-maker. Saturday mornings can also be a good time.

➠ If all else fails, go to Plan B—The Touching Program.

CHAPTER 5

Making Contact and Gaining Attention

In Chapter Four we addressed the first of the five skills critical to successful prospecting—the ability to identify the true decision-maker. In addition, we also discussed the importance of being persistent and tenacious when attempting to reach this key individual.

Our second critical skill will address how to gain the decision-maker's interest and attention when we finally connect.

Skill #2: The Ability to Make Contact with the Decision-Maker and Gain His or Her Attention.

Many books have been written about making "value statements" when you first talk to a potential customer, or the use of the traditional "elevator speech." I take great exception to that. In fact, the worst thing salespeople can do is start talking about themselves, their company, or their products and services until the customer or prospect is interested and ready to listen. As sales professionals, our job is to *get prospects interested.*

Tell prospects who you are and what you have to offer only *after* you have developed some interest and learned a little about their needs. Only then can you determine if what you have to offer could be a good fit.

Old school sales training taught salespeople that the purpose of the initial phone contact with the presumed decision-maker was to get the individual to agree to a face-to-face appointment. Unfortunately, many sales managers still teach and coach their salespeople that same old school philosophy: Get an appointment; get an appointment; get an appointment. They then hope the appointment is worthwhile.

I look at the telephone call much differently. As I mentioned earlier in this book:

"The Telephone Is Not A Tool To Make An Appointment . . .It *IS* An Appointment."

Based on that statement, the purpose of the call is:

- To determine potential for business.

- To begin building trust and understanding.

- To gain the other person's attention and interest.

Once we have one or more of those objectives accomplished, gaining a commitment for a face-to-face appointment is somewhat easier.

Unless you sell a product or service exclusively by telephone, you likely know the value of getting in front of your prospects if you want them to do business with you. On the other hand, salespeople have a much better chance of getting face-to-face with the prospect if they ask for the appointment *later* in the initial telephone conversation rather than making it the first thing discussed and the primary purpose of the call.

Many salespeople have been trained to start presenting the moment they make contact with the decision-maker. As such, they attempt to say everything about who they are and what they have to offer in one deep breath. Here's an example of what I mean:

> *"Hello, Jessica. My name is Patrick Willis with O'Toole's Printing. I'm calling to see if I could schedule an appointment to meet with you to discuss your company's printing needs. I promise not to take more than twenty minutes of your time; I know people in your position get very busy."*

> *"We've been in business now for almost twenty-five years in this area and we offer commercial printing, design services, direct marketing, business forms printing, and just about anything you could want in the way of printed materials."*

"I'm going to be in your area next week and I was wondering if I could schedule an appointment for us to get acquainted and discuss some of the ways we could save you money and be of service to your company. I'm wide open on next Tuesday or Thursday in the mornings but if you would prefer afternoon I would be available . . . on and on and on."

There's that "value statement" or "elevator speech" mentioned earlier. Just open up your mouth and tell the other person all about your company and services in one deep breath.

Most business professionals get very turned off by that approach. Often they are more turned off because the salesperson asked for an appointment before they have expressed any interest in the product or service. Remember, if they were already interested, they would be calling us.

Q: Why do salespeople use this somewhat outdated approach?

A: Fear of rejection, or it's just the way they've always done it.

The salesperson is often thinking: "I don't want to hear them tell me they are not interested, so if I just throw everything we have to offer at them in one deep breath, maybe something will hit the mark." They hope something they say will pique the customer's interest enough to grant them an appointment. In reality, that very rarely happens.

Q: Why doesn't this approach work?

A: The prospective customer is generally not listening.

I once read that we speak at a rate of about one hundred forty to one hundred sixty words per minute, and we think at about six hundred words per minute. Because we think so much faster than we speak, the person you are addressing can easily tune you out if he or she is not interested in hearing what you have to say.

Instead of listening, the other person is already thinking of excuses or reasons to say "no" to your request for an appointment, or to cut you off and terminate the call. In essence, you have not gained the decision-maker's attention.

The old numbers game approach is no longer appropriate. Attempting to make a hundred calls to get two appointments, with the hopes of making one sale, is not only costly but also time consuming. This approach can often result in scheduling a lot of no-show appointments, meeting with the wrong person, finding out there is little or no potential for business, and worse, leading with price to get in the door.

The old "smiling and dialing" technique often does not include pre-qualifying of the opportunity because the emphasis is on one thing—getting an appointment. If you are calling on a Fortune 500 company and you sell a big-ticket product or service, you might do a lot of pre-qualifying. However, if you need five to ten appointments per week to stay on top of your sales numbers and you are not always calling on major corporations, you can't spend a lot of time researching company history, industry rankings, competition, and who's who.

As such, why would you want to meet with someone before you've established an interest in your product or service? In addition, how do you know for sure that you're even talking to the person who can make the decision to buy? And what happens to the ones who said "no" to your request for an appointment? Do you just give up?

Today, sales is much more consultative, strategic, and relationship driven. It's not about number of appointments; it's about having quality appointments. The cost of a face-to-face sales call today is so expensive that meeting with people just for the sake of getting in the door is not cost effective.

Superstar Sales Professionals monitor and manage their closing percentages very closely. They analyze:

- Percentage of appointments gained to calls made.

- Percentage of appointments resulting in an opportunity to present a quote or proposal.

- Percentage of quotes or proposals resulting in a sale.

Superstar Sales Professionals are always looking for ways to ensure they are calling on qualified prospects. Later we'll talk about how to make that happen.

First, let's review some truths about business-to-business prospecting we addressed earlier.

When we finally reach our decision-maker, would he or she prefer that we had not called? With very few exceptions the answer is **yes!**

Is the decision-maker initially interested in hearing what we have to say? The answer is almost always **no!**

Are we interrupting the person? Unless he or she has nothing better to do than take calls all day from salespeople, the answer is **yes!**

Welcome to the world of sales!

Selling is about the ability to influence. It's about reaching key decision-makers who are not initially interested in hearing what we have to say and *getting* them interested in hearing what we have to say. And you have about ten to fifteen seconds to make that happen once you get them on the telephone.

Before you make your next prospecting call, take a few seconds to mentally picture the person you are about to call. What was that person doing when the telephone rang? For sure, they were not sitting around waiting for your call. They will be working on their computer, reading or preparing a report, communicating with someone else in the office, or any one of a dozen other tasks. Your number one objective is to break their existing train of thought and get their attention.

Q: What should we say when we make telephone contact with the prospect for the first time?

A: As little as necessary to verify we are speaking to the appropriate person. Here's an example.

Verify the Decision-Maker

Prospect: "Good morning, this is Mark."

Salesperson: "Good morning, Mark. This is Lauren Douglas with Best Business Machines. Mark, I was given your name as the person who makes the decisions about where your company purchases business machines such as copiers, faxes, and printers. Do I have the right person?"

Now at this point you can expect a "yes," "no," or some variation. Here are some examples.

"Yes."

"Yes, but we don't need anything right now."

"No, that would Bill Johnson."

"Actually, several people get involved in those decisions."

We have two objectives here:

- Verify that we do in fact have the right person.

- Gain that person's attention. Beginning the dialog by verifying that we do have the right person hopefully will accomplish both objectives.

For now, let's focus on what the salesperson has just said rather than the prospect's response. The three critical points in those first ten to fifteen seconds are as follows:

#1: Begin with a strong, confident, and professional opening statement. This is your telephone "handshake," and we all know how important a good, firm handshake is in making a positive first impression.

Avoid terms like "you guys," "ya know," "yeah" and other similar slang. If you want business professionals to take you seriously, you can't speak with them like you would talk to your friends over beer and pizza on Friday night. Regardless of how good you feel you are when meeting face-to-face, if you sound unprofessional on the phone, you will lose credibility. You must make the effort to sound mature, polished, and professional.

Grammar, diction, energy level, and confidence are all important in gaining interest and attention. When speaking on the telephone, you can't use body language or eye contact to help you overcome weaknesses in how you speak. You must make sure your communication skills are up to the task at hand.

Another point: you can't sound apologetic. As mentioned earlier, you must sound *Confident, Professional,* and even *Important.* Too often when making prospecting calls salespeople sound like they are doing something they should not be doing and wish they could get out of.

Remember that you are not selling swampland in Florida or bogus stocks. If you have a product or service that might be valuable to the business you are calling, you need to sound believable. How can we influence others to listen to our message if we sound as if we should apologize for bothering them?

#2: Get on a first name basis. Most Americans do business on a first name basis. Those still using Mr., Mrs., or Miss when conducting business are clearly in the minority. The use of Mr., Mrs. and Miss may be proper social graces, but not necessarily business protocol.

Business cards today reflect first names and even nicknames. William often becomes "Bill," and Catherine may show her name as "Katie." And almost always we answer our phones and leave voice mail messages using our first name.

Think about what happens when Katie, a twenty-nine-year-old sales professional, contacts Jack Jones, a fifty-year-old decision-maker, and says:

> *"Good Morning Mr. Jones, my name is Katie, and I represent the Ace Corporation . . ."*

Who's in control now? Where has Katie positioned herself in the pecking order or in the food chain? Jack may immediately think Katie views herself and her position as subservient to his, which is not an enviable position for a consultative, relationship driven sales professional.

Get on a first name basis and don't ask permission. Just do it. Rarely will your decision prove to be wrong. In consultative, relationship selling, you never want your prospect to view you as subservient. Instead, you want him to view you as the consultant, the advisor, and the product or service expert.

There are some exceptions, however. Always use professionally earned designations and titles, such as Doctor, General, and Reverend. And when addressing business professionals from other countries, you are much safer using Mr. and Mrs., as many European and Asian business cultures are more formal than our own.

Also, avoid statements like, "And, how are you today?" or "How ya doing?" At least don't say them the first time you speak to a prospective client. It reeks of "Tillie Telemarketer."

Remember "Tillie"? These were the people who would call you at home during the dinner hour and attempt to sell you magazine subscriptions, waterproofing for your basement, car insurance, etc. They always started the call the same way:

> *Tillie: "Hello, is this Mrs. Johnson?"*

> *Homeowner: "Yes"*

Tillie: "And how are you doing this evening?"

#3: Finish verifying the decision-maker with a question. And this will be one of the few occasions when a closed-ended question is preferred. You are seeking a "yes" or "no" answer. For example:

"Allen, I was told you are the person who makes the decisions regarding office furniture needs for your company. Is that true?" or, *"Is that correct?"* or, *"Is my information accurate?"*

You control the conversation's direction when you finish the verification with a question. If you don't, the other person will direct where the conversation goes. And most people will not lie and say they are the decision-maker when they are not, which is one reason the verification is so important. It confirms we do have the right person and does much to gain his or her attention.

Also, on a first contact, don't ask "Is this a good time?" or, "Do you have a minute?" Until you have developed at least some rapport, ninety-nine percent of the time, the prospect will use that question as an opportunity to get rid of you. It's okay not to ask if they have a minute. In business-to-business selling, if the prospective customer takes your call you can **assume permission** to talk at that time.

If you sense you've caught the person at a bad time, or he or she tells you it's a bad time, then reschedule the call. (We'll address that in Chapter Seven.) Continuing dialog when you know the timing is not good for the prospect is pushy and not professional. On the other hand, if the person doesn't mention that it's a bad time, then press on.

Speak in a warmly assertive manner. If you sound apologetic, nothing you say will have much impact. See the call as an opportunity, not an interruption, and that must clearly come through in your tone of voice.

Q: Okay, what happens next? What if I have the wrong person?

A: Back out if you have the wrong person.

Earlier I mentioned an old sales saying: *"Don't take no from a person who can't say yes."* Remember that phrase!

You must make sure you are talking to the person who makes the decisions. If you have not reached the right person and you allow the conversation to continue, you may find yourself in conversation with someone who may not make the final decision but can influence the person who does.

Let's assume you have reached Patrick, your presumed decision-maker, and when he responds to your question he says, *"No I'm not the right person."* You, however, continue discussing the purpose of your call, and he tells you that Daniel is the one who makes the final decisions but he does not think Daniel would be interested. He says:

"Daniel uses XYZ Company, and they give us very good service. I don't think he would be interested in making a change at this time."

Now you have backed yourself into a corner. If you opt to ignore his comment and call Daniel, you may very well have made an enemy of Patrick. And if Patrick has any influence regarding Daniel's decisions, you may have lost before you had a chance to win. Personally, I would rather not take that risk. Instead, I would back out gracefully and then attempt to get to the right person.

> *Salesperson: "Hello Earl, this is Jessica Thomas with Johnson Rentals. Earl, I was told you make the decisions regarding light equipment rentals for the construction crews. Is my information correct?"*

> *Prospect: "No it's not. I only approve the invoices for payment and make sure we apply the costs to the right project."*

> *Salesperson: "I'm sorry; I was given the wrong information. Earl, who should I be talking to?"*

Don't encourage extraneous conversation at this point. Politely attempt to get the appropriate name and move on. If you are not able to reach the true decision-maker, you can always go back to this person for additional information at a later date.

On occasion we'll run into multiple decision-maker situations. When this happens, just continue forward. If you've made contact with one of the decision-makers, treat that person as if he or she had full authority. Don't probe to determine which of the group is "top dog," at least for now.

At this point, we are not attempting to close a sale. We are prospecting to determine potential for business and get our foot in the door. Once we are able to get in the door, determining which one of the group carries the most clout is generally not that difficult. For now let's focus on this person. However, do so *only* if you have determined he or she is at least one of the decision-makers.

Before we close this chapter, here are a few more examples to consider when making contact and verifying the decision-maker.

"Good morning Eric, this is Wendy Gomez with Preferred Uniforms. I understand that you make the decisions relative to the warehouse uniform service. Is that correct?"

"Hi Jacob, Dennis Widmayer with Final Touch Construction. I was told you're responsible for decisions about sealing and finishing the concrete floors in the new store. Am I talking to the right person?"

"Angie, my name is Bud, and I'm with Computer Care Services. It's my understanding that you make all decisions regarding purchasing and repair of laptops for the sales staff. Is my information accurate?"

Q: What happens after we verify the decision-maker?

A: Ask for the business.

We'll discuss how to do that in the next chapter.

Key Points

The purpose of the prospecting call is to:

➠ Determine potential for business.

➠ Begin building trust and understanding.

➠ Gain the other person's attention and interest.

Monitor and manage your closing percentages:

➠ Appointments gained compared to calls made.

➠ Percentage that resulted in the opportunity to present a quote or proposal.

➠ Quotes or proposals resulting in a sale.

➠ When prospecting, most decision-makers we reach will not be glad we've called; they wish we would go away. Yes, we are interrupting them. Welcome to the world of sales.

➠ Begin with a strong, confident, and professional opening statement. This is your handshake.

➠ Get on a first name basis unless the use of a professionally earned designation is more appropriate. (Doctor, General, Rabbi, Professor, etc.)

➠ When making your first contact with the decision-maker, refrain from asking, "How are you doing?" We don't want to sound like "Tillie Telemarketer."

➠ Finish verifying the decision-maker with a question that requires a "yes" or "no" answer. Examples are: "Is that true?" "Is that correct?" "Do I have the right person?"

➠ If the prospect takes your call, assume you have permission to talk to him or her. Do not ask for permission.

➠ Back out if you have the wrong person. *Don't take no from a person who can't say yes.*

CHAPTER 6

Ask for the Business

Now we're ready for the third of the five skills critical to successful prospecting.

Skill #3: The Ability to Confidently Ask for the Business.

This skill may represent one of the most dramatic differences in the way you previously learned how to sell, and one of the more difficult skills to master.

I've met many salespeople who have been in sales for years who were not comfortable or competent at asking for the business.

Let's look at some examples of how to ask for the business.

"Joe, I'm calling because our company would love the opportunity to do business with your firm. What's the best way for us to position ourselves to make that happen?"

"United Plus is an industry leader in the area of distribution software development and we would value the opportunity to work with your organization. How do we go about being considered?"

"Tom, we feel that our business banking services fit well with companies similar to your own in size and business type. What

would be the first step for us to have an opportunity to earn your business?"

How can we ever be successful in sales if we can't ask for the business?

Don't hint, suggest, or beg. **Ask for the business.** We are not calling to see if we can help them out, or to see if they need anything, or to get acquainted and learn more about their company. We're calling because we would like an opportunity to do business with them. Tell the truth.

Is that wrong or too direct?

If you think it is, then I suggest you close this book right now and spend your time putting together a resume targeted to a non-sales position. Would *you* attempt to run a sales-driven company with salespeople who could not comfortably and confidently ask for the business?

Let's look at how this flows when we put it together with verifying the decision-maker:

> *Prospect: "Good morning, this is Heather."*
>
> *Salesperson: "Good morning Heather, this is Patti Wilson with Computer Services. I was given your name as the person who makes the decisions about PC maintenance and computer training at your company. Is my information correct?"*
>
> *Prospect: "Yes, but right now we have a contract with another company."*
>
> *Salesperson: "I understand and I appreciate your honesty. Heather, we'd like the opportunity to do business with your organization if and when you might be open to making a comparison. How can we position ourselves to be considered?"*

Was the salesperson pushy, obnoxious, and high-pressure? Not at all.

How do you think a prospect feels about a salesperson who calls and (A) gets to the point, and (B) tells the truth about why he or she is calling? I would be greatly surprised if you did not find the results extremely positive. A more direct or assertive approach is honest and up-front and will not be offensive as long as your tone is warm and friendly.

Don't be concerned with the responses you will get when you ask for the business; we'll cover that in detail in our next chapter. For now, here are key points to remember when asking for the business.

Assume the Need

Don't talk yourself out of making the call because you're not sure if they use or need the product or service you sell. If you determine this is not a good prospect, turn it into a public relations or "PR" call. Here's an example:

> *Salesperson: "Erica, Employee Placement provides temporary staff services in a wide range of areas including light industrial. How could we become the company you would contact when those needs arise?"*

> *Prospect: "Katie, we have not had the need to use a temp for over five years. We used to when we did quarterly inventory, but that's all done by computer now. We just never have the need."*

> *Salesperson: "Well I appreciate your taking the time to speak with me today, and if your situation ever changes, I hope you'll let us know."*

Our salesperson, Katie, determined the potential for business was too little to justify further effort and chose to turn this into a PR call and move on.

She can always place this account in her contact management program or follow-up file and call again in six to twelve months to see if anything has changed. For now, she has no reason to continue dialog. We're looking for accounts having some potential for business. Spending time on accounts that do not can waste a lot of valuable time, energy, and money.

State the True Purpose of the Call

Don't lie, hint, or skirt the issue. Tell the truth. Here are some examples of **ineffective** ways to ask for the business.

> *"I was just calling to see if you might be interested in hearing about a special we have going on at this time?"*

(Too passive, almost apologetic.)

> *"Would it be possible to take a minute of your time and ask a few questions? I just wanted to see if there might be some areas where we could be of service."*

(We're begging and setting ourselves up for a "no.")

"I was calling to see if you would like to receive some information about our company and the products we offer?"

(Not even close. We could get a high school kid to make these calls.)

"I was wondering if you would allow us to come in a give you a price quote?"

(This is selling price. Superstar Sales Professional never lead with price.)

Breaking down "Asking for the Business" into these three segments might help you more easily master the skill. The three segments are:

- The Warmer

- The Want

- The Ask

The Warmer

The *Warmer* is the first thing we say after we have verified we have the decision-maker. Let's look at some examples:

> *Salesperson: "Joe, it's my understanding that you make the decisions when it comes to logo and ad specialty items for your company. Is that true?"*
>
> *Prospect: "Yes"*

Examples of warmers:

- "Great!"

- "Thanks for taking my call"

- "Well I appreciate your taking my call"

- "I'm glad I was able to reach you."

The *Warmer* is a way to ease into the purpose of the call in a more conversational and non-threatening manner. The last thing we want to do is sound canned and rigid. People buy from people, not machines. As such, we need to focus on building rapport when attempting to gain their business.

As we discussed earlier, you may get more than just "yes." You may get a "yes but." When that happens your warmer needs to acknowledge the objection as well as ease into asking for the business. Here are some examples:

> *Salesperson: "Joe, it's my understanding that you make the decisions when it comes to logo and ad specialty items for your company. Is that true? "*

> *Prospect: "Yes, but right now we don't need anything."*

Warmers to consider:

- *"Well I appreciate your honesty."*

- *"Thanks for sharing that with me."*

- *"I understand."*

- *"I see."*

Here again, the Warmer is simply a way to ease into dialog in a warm and conversational manner. It also tells the prospective customer that you are listening.

The Want

When training salespeople, hands down, this is where they struggle the most. If I'm training a rookie, the struggle is generally due to a lack of experience. The new salesperson is trying to find the right combination of words to fit his or her style.

When training the more seasoned sales professional, it's more about breaking old habits. Some people are so programmed to ask for the appointment that changing from that to asking for the business takes a lot of practice.

The most difficult salespeople to work with, however, are the ones who feel this is too direct and borders on pushy. These same reps will admit that when they hear others say "The Want," it sounds professional and not at all pushy. However, because of their "fear of offending," they find it difficult to do themselves.

This is where practicing with a tape-recorder is so valuable, and we'll discuss that in detail when we address "Drills for Skills" later in this book. In the meantime, here are some examples of "The Want":

> *"I'm calling because our company would like to be your source for whatever office supply needs you have."*

> *"Lisa, the purpose of my call is that Dana's Commercial Flooring would like a chance to win the flooring contract for your upcoming building renovation."*

> *"The reason I'm calling, Dan, is that we would love the opportunity to do business with your firm."*

> *"Jason, my company, Ace Computers, would like to be considered for all of your PC repair, maintenance, and network needs."*

The Ask

Once you have shared with the customer the purpose of your call, "The Want," we now need to ask for the opportunity. And we do that for two reasons.

The first reason is to encourage the prospective customer to talk. When *we* are talking, *they* are in control. As such, we need to get them engaged in conversation as soon as possible. The best way to do that is to ask an **open-ended question** that will encourage a response other than "yes" or "no." Here are some examples:

> *"I'm calling because our company would like to be your source for whatever office supply needs you have. What's the best way for us to position our company to be considered?"*

> *"Lisa, the purpose of my call is that Dana's Commercial Flooring would like a chance to win the flooring contract for your upcoming building renovation. How do we go about getting an opportunity to present a proposal?"*

> *"The reason I'm calling, Dan, is that we would love the opportunity to do business with your firm. How can we interest you in at least taking a look at what we have to offer?"*

"Jason, my company, Ace Computers, would like to be considered for all of your PC repair, maintenance, and network needs. What can my company do to earn that opportunity?"

The second reason for "The Ask" is to draw out the first objection or point of resistance. **Yes, we need to draw out the objection.** The sooner we know what, if any, objections exist to doing business with us, the sooner we can address it.

We can't avoid objections, ignore them, or make them go away. Thinking prospects will say something like, "Come over and let's talk. I'll put the coffee on," is just not realistic. Most likely we will hear an objection and we will need to know how to address it. But we can't do that until we know what the objection is. Again, how to do that is the focus of our next chapter.

After "The Ask," listen for the response. **Don't say a word.** Allow your prospect the opportunity to hit you with the first point of resistance and/or the objection.

Learning to confidently and competently ask for the business will open doors and expose opportunities you never knew were there. Just think of all the different ways you can use this skill.

Here are a few examples:

Salesperson: "Allison, I understand from Casey that you take care of truck rentals for the warehouse. We're currently working with him at your Circleville location and we'd like to have the contract for this warehouse. What would be your requirements for us to be considered?" Scripps ?

Salesperson: "Good morning, Richard. My name is Jacob Rogers and I'm with Executive Telecom. I recently read that your company is starting a branch office in our area and I was calling to see how we could be considered for your telephone and wireless needs. Richard, what would be the first step for us to compete for that business?"

Salesperson: "Hi Erin, this is Lauren with Commercial Furnishings. I just heard that you won the design contract for the new Children's Hospital wing and we'd love to have a chance to provide the patient care furniture. What do we need to do to have a shot at working with you on this project?"

Becoming confident and competent in asking for the business takes time and practice. However, when it comes to prospecting for business it can be the single most important skill you master.

Now let's look at a telephone prospecting cold-call from the beginning:

Receptionist: "Good Afternoon, Mitchell's Real Estate. How may I help you?"

Salesperson: "Good afternoon, this is Brenda Willis with Metro Security Systems. I have a packet of information I need to forward to the person who makes the decisions regarding security alarm systems for your model home offices. Who should I send this to?"

Receptionist: "That would be Simon Elliott."

Salesperson: "And for my file, what is Simon's position with the company?"

Receptionist: "He's the director of operations."

Salesperson: "By chance would he happen to have a minute to talk to me?"

Receptionist: "I'm not sure; I'll connect you to his office."

Prospect: "This is Simon."

Salesperson: "Hello Simon. My name is Brenda Willis and I'm with Metro Security Systems. I understand you're the person responsible for decisions regarding security alarm systems for your model home offices. Have I reached the right person?"

Prospect: "Yes, but we have a company we use for that service and we're all set right now."

Salesperson: "I understand and I appreciate your honesty. Simon, I'm calling because our company would like the opportunity to be considered for those needs. What could we do to interest you in at least taking a look at what we have to offer?"

Assume the need, state the purpose of the call, and then listen.

I've mentioned this before, but it warrants mentioning one more time: When you are talking, your prospects or customers are in control, as they can think much faster than you can talk. When you can get them talking, you are in control. And our goal is just that: Getting them to talk.

What they will say and how we plan to address it are the topics of our next chapter, so let's move on.

Key Points

➡ You can't be successful in sales if you can't confidently and competently ask for the business.

➡ Always assume the need. If you determine later this is not a good prospect, you can turn the call into a PR call rather than a prospecting call and back out.

➡ State the true purpose of the call. Don't lie, hint, or skirt the issue. Ask for the business.

➡ Break down asking for the business into three segments: The Warmer, The Want, and The Ask.

➡ The two reasons for the "Ask." (A) Encourage the prospect to talk. (B) Draw out the first objection.

➡ After the "Ask" do not say a word. Wait for their response.

➡ Assume the need, state the purpose of the call, and then listen.

CHAPTER 7

Addressing Objections and Resistance

We've addressed how to identify the decision-maker, make contact and verify he or she is the right person, and then ask for the business. What happens next? We move into the next skill:

Skill #4: The Ability to Effectively Address the First Objection or Resistance to Your Call.

Once we have asked for the business and have stopped talking, we can expect our prospect to give a response. At this point, wouldn't you love to hear something like: "Wow, I can't believe your timing. Come on over!"

While there is something to be said for timing, rarely will you ever hear such a positive greeting when making telephone prospecting calls. Typically, you'll hear something similar to one or more of the following objections:

❑ Send me some information and I'll keep it on file.

❑ We're satisfied with Valley View, our current supplier.

❑ You caught me at a bad time; I'm too busy to talk.

❑ We don't need anything right now.

❑ We had a bad experience with your company and I'm not sure we would do business with you again.

❑ We don't have any budget for that right now.

❑ You're too late; we just signed a contract for everything we need.

❑ You're way too early; we're not ready to look at that yet.

❑ I'm not familiar with your company.

❑ You would have to give us better pricing than we're currently getting.

❑ My brother-in-law is in the business and we get everything at cost.

At this point in the prospecting call the decision-maker is generally not interested in talking to you; if that person were he or she would have called you. Right now, the decision-maker's objective is to get you to go away. Some are more polite than others, but they still are saying the same thing: "Go away."

The Un-Comfort Zone

We agreed earlier that we are probably interrupting prospects. People at work are not usually sitting around playing solitaire on their computers or in the break room reading a novel. They're busy, and they often view sales calls as interruptions. Our job is to turn that around and get the prospect interested in hearing what we have to say.

While business-to-business sales professionals admit they hear objections all the time, many who fail in sales do so because of their inability to effectively address objections. To some, hearing the first objection or point of resistance can be so terrifying that they refuse to prospect.

Hearing, *"Look, I'm doing business with someone else and I see no reason to change,"* can be more frightening to some than the fear of not making their sales goal and even losing their job.

Why are we so uncomfortable with the first objection we hear when prospecting either face-to-face or by telephone? Consider the following two reasons.

1. Some salespeople have never had to prospect for new business, but for some reason that has changed, and now they do and it represents change. Existing account business may have dried up, or the salesperson is simply not making enough money and needs more business.

I have met a number of salespeople who were good at hanging on long enough for other salespeople to retire, move on, or pass on, and they acquired their existing accounts. These salespeople were able to make a living without having to prospect. However, many of those same salespeople began to hurt when their accounts started drying up in a tough economy and they did not have the necessary prospecting skills to replace them. A tough economy does not mean *no* business; it means *less* business and you have to hunt to find it.

Early in my business, one of my clients told me he was struggling with how to get his salespeople to go after new business. They sold a high-priced product that had been in big demand for a number of years.

During the good years, the company regularly received calls almost daily from prospective clients who wanted to schedule appointments with salespeople. Orders for the product came in by telephone, e-mail, or fax, and they were totally unsolicited. A salesperson with even reasonably good product knowledge could make an upper six-figure income without the need to prospect.

Eventually, however, customers began to view the product as a commodity. Competition was fierce, and profit margins declined. For the first time, the company needed to aggressively prospect for new business. His salespeople, however, were still waiting for the next request for a proposal or for the company to assign them a new account.

The salespeople's resistance to prospecting was so intense that it became necessary for the client to dismiss several of his senior salespeople and begin building a sales team with new hires who were willing and eager to learn how to prospect for business.

2. Some salespeople lack training and skill development. For example, let's look at how unskilled salespeople commonly address objections.

> *Prospect: "Send me some information in the mail and I'll keep it on file."*

> *Salesperson: "I'll do that, and if it's okay with you I'll call back next week to see if you have any questions. Now let me verify that address. I show 2021 E. Hudson Street . . ."*

What makes this response so weak and ineffective?

When the prospect suggested sending information, it was a way for him to get the salesperson off the phone. When we call, most of the time a prospective customer initially wants us to "go away." And in this scenario, that's exactly what the salesperson did; he went away. The salesperson was far too accommodating and did just what the prospect wanted. Equally as bad, the salesperson learned absolutely nothing but the correct mailing address.

Any reasonably experienced salesperson knows the prospect does not really want the information, but the salesperson lacks the skills to know how to address the objection or "go away" in a more effective manner.

The call just highlighted was worthless, and we could have hired a high school student to make that call for all the information we learned. We sure did not need a professional salesperson. And in all probability, the salesperson will send something by mail that will most likely end up in the prospect's wastebasket.

While we're on the subject of what this unskilled salesperson might send, that same salesperson will call back a week later, and if he's lucky enough to get the decision-maker on the telephone again, here is what you might hear:

"I wanted to follow-up on the information I sent to you. Did you get it?"

How weak is that? Is it our job to make sure the post office delivered the mail? If we're going to follow-up on mail, we should at least use a more powerful opening statement, such as:

> *"I wanted to follow-up on the information I sent. How did it look to you?"*

Or,

> *"I wanted to follow-up on the information I sent. What if any questions did you have regarding the product?"*

Or,

> *"I wanted to follow-up on the information I sent. What were your thoughts about the program we're offering?"*

Always assume the prospect received your information, and assume he or she read it. If the prospect did not receive it or read it, he or she will tell you. The phrase "Did you get it?" is very weak and ineffective because it does not enable you to gather any new, relevant information.

Here is another example of an ineffective way to address an objection:

> *Prospect: "We're satisfied with Valley View, our current supplier."*

*Salesperson: "I'm familiar with them, and they are a good company, but I'm confident that if I could show you how our program could save you time and money I know you would want to at least . . ."*yackety, yackety, yak."

Rule number one: Never brag about your competition. Why would you want to validate that your prospect has made a wise choice in who they bought from?

While I agree we should never make negative remarks about the competition, I'm not going to sing their praises. It's not necessary. You can acknowledge that you are familiar with the company without saying anything about how you feel about them.

However, even worse than singing the competitor's praises, the salesperson went into a "sales pitch" when confronted with the objection. I call this the *"but, but, but"* response. The salesperson was not willing to address the objection because he was focused on his own agenda. He was more concerned about what he wanted to say rather than responding to what he had heard.

Here is one final example of an ineffective way to address the first objection when prospecting:

Prospect: "We don't have any budget for new equipment right now."

Salesperson: "Well, is it okay if I check back in a couple of months, or do you know when a budget might be approved?"

Clearly the salesperson has sent the message that she is focused on one thing: when will the prospect have money to spend so she can plan to call back at that time. What kind of a message does that send to a potential customer? And again, what will we learn other than when they might have a budget allocated?

Q: How can we avoid objections and resistance when prospecting?

A: You can't and you shouldn't. Embrace the objection; don't try to run from it. Learning how to effectively address objections is key to having a successful career in sales.

When effectively addressing objections, you won't always get what you want, but overall you will win more business, more often, and with less effort. Having good selling skills means knowing what to do, how to do it, and when.

Once we have "asked for the business" and been hit with the first objection, we have three choices for our next move.

- Give up and go away.

- Push back with *"but, but, but"* and *"talk, talk, talk"* and risk making the prospect angry.

- Listen and then transition to an ***open-ended*** question to encourage dialog and develop trust and rapport.

To the Superstar Sales Professional, options one and two are not acceptable. Option three is where we want to go. Here's why:

We want to encourage the prospect to talk. If we can get the prospect to talk to us, even if for only a short time, two things can happen:

- We have an opportunity to gain information that can be invaluable in determining the overall potential for business and even time frames.

- When you can get people to talk about *their* needs and *their* issues, the opportunity to build trust and rapport increases dramatically. Selling is not about *telling* . . . it's about *asking.*

Listen . . . then transition to an open-ended question.

Here are some examples:

> *Prospect: "Send me some information in the mail. I'll keep it on file."*
>
> *Salesperson: "I would be happy to. Eric, when do you anticipate that you'll need to replace or update your current audio visual equipment?"*
>
> ———————————————————
>
> *Prospect: "We're satisfied with Valley View, our current supplier."*
>
> *Salesperson: "I'm familiar with Valley View. Mark, when was*

the last time you made a comparison between their products and services and what another office products dealer might have to offer?"

Prospect: "We don't have any budget for new equipment right now."

Salesperson: "I understand and I appreciate your honesty. Maria, if budget were not an issue and funds were available, what would be at the top of your list to purchase?"

In each of the three objections, you will find the same techniques. The salesperson "listened and then transitioned to an open-ended question." Our objective is to 1) Encourage dialog, and 2) Develop interest and rapport.

So where do we ultimately want to go in this call? And how long do we continue to talk?

Let's look at a call that takes us beyond that first point of resistance:

Prospect: "We don't have any budget for new equipment right now."

Salesperson: "I understand and I appreciate your honesty. If budget were not an issue and funds were available, what would be at the top of your list to purchase?"

Prospect: "Probably a couple of new mowers and another flat-bed truck, but it's a moot point right now. We don't have the money."

Salesperson: "Maria, may I ask what is driving the need for the new mowers and truck?"

Prospect: "Well, we need the truck because we're growing and we're having to rent flatbeds too often to get tree and shrub deliveries to our crews. The mowers would replace equipment that's old and needs replacing."

Salesperson: "Well at least part of your need for new equipment is because you're growing and that's good. I know you said there was no budget for equipment right now, but it seems like at some point, you'll have to purchase at least the new mowers. How would you feel about giving me an hour of your time to take a look at what you're using and what we have to offer and at least give you some ballpark pricing and equipment options to think about? Then when you are ready, you'll have a feel for what might work best and pricing information. How does that sound to you?"

Prospect: "Not too good. I'm so busy right now and unless we have a mower that can't be repaired, I don't want to even look at any new equipment until end of second quarter next year. That's when our large steel building is paid off and we'll be a little less tight with money. We can get by with what we have until then."

Salesperson: "Maria, I understand and I respect your decision. What can I do to make sure that when you are ready to look at new equipment, we can at least be considered?"

Prospect: "Stay in touch and send me a little information about what you carry and include your business card. If anything changes we'll let you know."

The Superstar Sales Professionals would say this was a *"great telephone appointment."* Look at what the salesperson has learned about Maria and the potential for business.

The Superstar Sales Professional knows that Maria needs two mowers and a flatbed truck. More important, he or she knows why and approximately when the prospect expects to have the budget to make new equipment purchases.

And because our sales professional did not push hard for an appointment but rather focused on getting the prospect to talk about *her* needs and *her* time frames, the salesperson has built some rapport, gained some quality information, and has a very qualified lead to put in the prospecting funnel. To the Superstar Sales Professional, this is not the end, but rather the beginning.

By continuing to stay in touch and nurturing the relationship until the time is right, our sales professional should expect at least a shot at the business. We'll address more on how to do that in our next chapter when we address "The Touching Program."

Q: Will people always talk to you and give you good information?

A: Absolutely not. However, most will if you ask questions about their needs and their business and talk less about your company and what you want and have to offer.

I'm always amazed how many sales managers role-play objections with their sales staff and play the "prospect from hell" that Moses could not get in to see. That is not real world.

In business-to-business sales, if you make contact with ten prospects and you are a skilled professional who knows how to effectively address objections, you will rarely get more than one or two who play hardball and refuse to talk to you. While we can't get them all, we will improve our chances for success when we have good selling skills.

Let's go back to "old school selling" where the purpose of the call to Maria would have been solely for the purpose of getting a face-to-face appointment. Here is how that might have sounded:

Salesperson: "Maria, I was calling today to see if I could schedule an appointment to meet with you and learn a little about your landscaping business. We sell equipment to commercial landscaping companies all over the country, and I would love to meet with you and show you what we have to offer."

Prospect: "This would not be a good time; we don't have any budget for new equipment right now."

Salesperson: "Okay. Well one of things we have to offer is a very cost effective leasing program that can save you money and at the same time, keep your payments very low. Would you be interested in considering a good leasing program?"

Prospect: "I might, but right now we have no budget for purchasing or leasing. We're not going to buy anything new until next year."

Salesperson: "Well, when would be a good time for me to get back to you?"

Prospect: "Why don't you send me some information about what you have to offer and when we're ready to start looking at equipment, we'll let you know."

In this scenario the salesperson was focused on his or her agenda, which was getting an appointment. As such, all the salesperson learned was that there is currently no budget and they would not be buying anything until next year.

Going back to our assumption that the first objection or resistance we confront when prospecting is an attempt to get us to go away, what happens when the prospect does not open up and talk, and instead you get *another* "Go Away?"

When that happens, you go away. Trying to force a conversation with a prospective customer who, for whatever the reason, does not want to talk to you is high pressure selling, and in my view, totally unprofessional and unacceptable.

Let's look at a professional way to ease out of a call when the prospect is not going to talk to you. After asking for their business we hear:

> *Prospect: "Drop me some information in the mail and I'll take a look at it. Right now we're all set."*

> *Salesperson: "I would be happy to do that. James, who do you purchase your safety equipment and supplies from now?"*

> *Prospect: "There are a couple companies we use. Just send me some information and I'll take a look at it."*

> *Salesperson: "Will do and thanks for taking my call. I'll include my business card so feel free to let me know if you have any questions."*

If you opt to send something before attempting another try at talking to this person, keep it short and simple. Do not send a ton of information that the person will likely pitch. Send your business card and maybe a brief note about your company or a brochure. What you really want to do is attempt to reach the prospect in a week or two and try again to develop interest and rapport.

When prospects are abrupt, a number of things can be going on in their life. They may have just lost one of their best employees. They may have found out they did not get a promotion they were expecting. They may have started the morning with a flat tire on the way to work. We may not know why people are sometimes abrupt and not interested in talking to us, but our job is to turn that around if at all possible. So going away should be a temporary move, not necessarily permanent.

In a week or two call the prospect again and see if things are any different. Here's an example of how that call might sound:

Salesperson: "Hello James. This is Dean with Ace Safety Supplies. I called about a week ago and I think I had caught you at a bad time; you sounded rushed. I was hoping to have a minute to talk to you. Is this a better time?"

In our second attempt we may find James just as rushed and abrupt as we did the first time. Or, we may find he is receptive to our call and willing to talk for a few minutes. However, we will never know until we try.

As we begin to close this chapter, let's look at how our Superstar Sales Professional might tackle each of the following objections he or she might hear after asking for the business. Some we've already addressed, but we'll do it again using a different response.

✓ **Send me some information and I'll keep it on file.**

I would be happy to. John, who currently handles your advertising promotions?

✓ **We're satisfied with Valley View, our current supplier.**

I understand. How long have you been buying from them?

✓ **You caught me at a bad time; I'm too busy to talk.**

I'm sorry I did not mean to catch you at a bad time. Lisa, when would be a better time for me to call back?

✓ **We don't need anything right now.**

Jason, when do you anticipate that might change?

✓ **We had a bad experience with your company and I'm not sure we would do business with you again.**

I'm really sorry to hear that. Jessica, how could my company redeem themselves and earn a second chance?

✓ **We don't have any budget for that right now.**

Ann, if budget were not an issue, what do you see your equipment needs being?

✓ **You're too late; we just signed a contract for everything we need.**

John, I regret not calling you sooner. What do we need to do to be positioned for consideration on your next project?

✓ **You're way too early; we're not ready to look at that yet.**

Well Joe, I'm glad I'm too early and not too late. What do we need to do to be positioned for consideration when you're ready to look at the security needs for your new warehouse?

✓ **I'm not familiar with your company.**

Well GreenTree Construction has been in office complex development for over eighteen years in the southern part of the state, and we've just recently opened a division in this area. We offer top quality construction to client's specifications and we've enjoyed a good reputation for meeting customer's budgets and deadlines. Tim, when do you anticipate you'll be building your next facility?

✓ **You would have to give us better pricing than we're currently getting.**

Paul, let's assume we could give you very competitive pricing. What other issues would impact your decision to change vendors that had nothing to do with price?

✓ **My brother-in-law is in the business and we get everything at cost.**

Move on. There is not enough potential for business to make this worth your effort.

Position Yourself for Future Success

So far we've talked about the need to identify the true decision-maker, verify we have the right person, ask for the business, and address the first objection or point of resistance.

However, this is still no guarantee that the prospect is going to give you an appointment or that you will have a shot at his or her business. Yes, it's a good start, but what if the prospective customer is just not interested in making a change at this time or really does not have any current needs? What do Superstar Sales Professionals do to position themselves for the future?

We'll address that in our next chapter. Let's move on.

Key Points

➠ Those who fail at sales often do so because of their inability to effectively address objections.

➠ The reason many salespeople are not effective at addressing objections when prospecting is (A) In the past, they never had to prospect, and (B) Lack of training and skill development.

➠ Never brag about your competition. Why would you want to validate that your prospect has made a wise choice in who they bought from? At the same time, never make negative comments about them either.

➠ Learning how to effectively address objections is key to having a successful career in sales.

➠ Getting the prospect to talk can give us invaluable information and an opportunity to build trust and rapport.

➠ Selling is not about *telling* . . . it's about *asking*.

➠ When addressing an objection: Listen . . . then transition to an open-ended question.

CHAPTER 8

The Touching Program

A sk any salesperson, whether a rookie or seasoned professional, what he or she believes is the toughest challenge to being successful in sales, and overwhelmingly the answer will be: Getting an appointment with the right person. In some situations, you may spend weeks, months, or even years to make that happen. That's why you must have the following skill:

Skill #5: The Ability to Position Yourself for the Future When *Now* is Not an Option.

Earlier we mentioned the days of "smiling and dialing" and how that approach is no longer the most effective way to go after business. Making one hundred calls or "dials" to get a few appointments and perhaps one or two sales is just not the way sales professionals work today. At least that's not how Superstar Sales Professionals work. Why? Because such a method does not support an action plan for the ones who say "No" to your request for an appointment, or the ones you are just never able to reach.

The theory behind "smiling and dialing" is that if you keep calling and recycling the same names eventually you will connect at the right time, with the right person, and he or she will have a need for your products or service. While in some cases that happens, the salesperson has no strategic advantage over anyone else who is "smiling and dialing" the same prospect.

Q: So, what are the options when you've tried and just can't reach the right person, or you reach the right person and he or she won't agree to meet with you?

A: The Touching Program. I sometimes refer to it as "professional flirting."

Remember when you were in high school and you were attracted to someone who was going steady with another person? Did you stop flirting with that person just because he or she was already going with someone else? Of course not.

You knew when the bell rang to change classes how fast you had to run and in what direction to have thirty seconds to see that person, smile, say "Hi," and still get to your class on time.

You knew exactly where he or she sat in study hall, and you always found a way to sit close by.

You knew where that person went for pizza on Friday nights after the game, and you and your friends always seemed to show up at the same place.

Your goal was to make sure that if something changed in his or her current relationship, that he or she would know who you were. You positioned yourself perfectly for a first date.

Now let's see how that same approach might work when trying to get a prospective customer to consider doing business with us.

The Touching Program

If you want to gain an edge and set yourself apart when attempting to win over prospective customers, utilize a "Touching Program." What's a Touching Program? It's a system that enables you to make contact with your prospect on a regular basis and in a variety of ways that will ultimately "brand" you and make sure the prospect knows who *you* are.

"You can't win if you are not in the game," and making contact with prospects on a regular basis is critical to converting prospects to customers.

First, you need to allocate two hours, every two weeks, to keep your program up to date. Your Touching Program is not about skill; it's about discipline.

You must have access to a computer-based contact management program. You can choose from many these days, and they all allow you to keep good notes, thus making follow-up contact easy, timely, and systematic, which is critical to the success of your program.

Next you need to begin filling your Touching Program funnel with *qualified leads* that fall into one of two categories:

❑ Potential to be a good account or sale at some point in time, but right now there is no need and/or money.

❑ They are doing business with a competitor and not open to changing or making a comparison at this time.

Before we move on, let's take another look at what we've determined are *qualified leads*.

1. Potential to be a good account or sale at some point in time, but right now there is no need and/or money.

Untold numbers of sales are lost every day because the salesperson saw little value in pursuing a relationship with a prospective customer who was not ready to make a buying decision *now*.

These salespeople often have appointment or sales quotas to meet, and their focus is on finding prospects who are ready to buy *now* or who are at least willing to meet with them *now*. They may be working hard, but not necessarily smart.

Later when those same prospects are ready to make a purchase, the salesperson who moved on without positioning herself gave the prospect no reason to remember her.

2. They are doing business with a competitor and not open to changing or making a comparison at this time.

Here again, sales are often lost because the salesperson is not willing to stay the course and compete with an existing relationship. His call reports often read: *"Not interested, currently does business with Valley View and happy. Try again in six months."*

Without an action plan to position himself for consideration during that time, his call report may state the same message again in six months.

If you are currently in sales, ask yourself one question: "How much business closes every day in my marketing area that I am not even being considered for?" If you are losing more business than you want to lose, a Touching Program can be a way to fix that. Here is how it works.

When we have been unable to gain an opportunity *now* with a *qualified* prospect, in lieu of badgering and trying to get the prospect to change his or her mind, back off and start positioning yourself for the future. And the key is *back off*, not give up. Here are a few examples of how that might sound:

> *Salesperson: "Joe, if you're satisfied with Valley View and not interested in changing at this time, I respect that. I'll check back now and then, but in the meantime, would you keep my business card on file and let me be the first person you call if you change you mind?"*

The majority of people will say "sure" or "yes" and even "I would be glad to," even if they do not really mean it. The salesperson's job then is to make sure they remember."

> *Salesperson: "Lisa, if you're not open to meeting with me now I understand. I'll touch base with you from time to time so that when you are ready for new equipment we might be considered. I'll send you my business card and some information about our products, but never hesitate to call if there is anything we can do for you."*

No pushing or badgering for the appointment. That might damage the relationship. Instead the salesperson told Lisa he or she would touch base from time to time, but for now, the salesperson is backing off.

> *Salesperson: "I understand about budgets and I know that until that changes you won't consider upgrading your telephone system. Jason, I would like to keep the door open in case that changes anytime soon, so I'll stay in touch. But, please feel free to give me a call if there is anything we can do for you."*

In all three scenarios the salesperson <u>told</u> the prospect he or she would stay in touch, which is far more effective than asking, *"Would it be okay if I checked back with you from time to time?"* Why risk being told, *"Don't call me, I'll call you."*

Important: In lieu of having to add another 500 or so pages to this book to provide examples of entire conversations between a salesperson and a prospective customer, you need to make the following assumption:

The scenarios just highlighted were the end of what might have been a lengthy conversation, and the salesperson had done an excellent job of doing all he or she could have done to gain the prospect's interest and an opportunity to win the business.

Never put a prospect in a Touching Program at the first sign of resistance; rather, do so only after you have done everything you could, short of high pressure, to turn things around in your favor.

So how can we touch base with prospects regularly without becoming a nuisance? And how often should we make contact to effectively position ourselves?

First, do not touch too frequently. Every six to eight weeks is generally enough for them to remember who you are and recognize your name and company, but not so much they will feel you are pestering and becoming a nuisance.

The key, however, is *how* you "touch." Most important is that you do not ask them to respond to any of your touches unless they chose to do so. If you leave a voice mail message, do not ask them to return your call.

Make it easy for them to catch your name, listen to what you have to say, and then hit delete. If you send an e-mail, do the same thing. Make it easy for the prospect to have nothing more to do than hit delete or throw something in the wastebasket.

The objective to a successful Touching Program is branding *you*. Companies brand companies; manufacturers brand products; *you* need to brand *you*. The prospect needs to know who you are.

How do we make that happen?

A follow-up phone call is a great way to touch. Keep it short. Tell them you are still very interested in having their business and to let you know if there is anything you can do for them. Here's an example of how that might sound:

Salesperson: "Hello, Lisa. This is Brian Smith with Cooper Industrial Equipment. We talked a couple of months ago and at that time you had some budget issues and were not ready to look at new equipment. I wanted to check back and say hello and ask if anything has changed since we last talked?"

Prospect: "Brian, it's not much better. We're still on a budget freeze and it does not look like it will change anytime soon. Our business is really slow right now."

Salesperson: "I understand, but I wanted to make sure you knew that we were still very interested in working with you when you're ready, and that you had not forgotten my name. Just feel free to let me know if there is anything I can do for you."

If the prospect seems to want to talk, go for it. If not, however, terminate the call quickly and do not push for more time. Remember, we are touching for the purpose of branding ourselves and making sure they know who we are. Push too hard too soon and we might close the door permanently.

Now you need to notate in your contact management program that you contacted that person on this date and what transpired. Then *immediately* set a date for the next touch.

Voicemail is another way to touch. Again, keep it short and reinforce that you want to do business with them. You might even mention an upcoming sale or a new product and then ask them to let you know if they are interested in having any additional information. Here is an example:

"Hello, Dana. This is Wendy Lewis with Office Services. Sorry we were not able to connect with each other but I know you're busy. I wanted to say hello and to let you know that we would still value an opportunity to do business with you folks, so I hope you'll not hesitate to call if there is anything we can do for you. I'm assuming you still have my business card but just in case my number is 555-1231. And by the way, if you are in the market for any high quality color printers, the new XL15 model is now out and we're hearing nothing but rave reviews about it. Let me know if you are interested in any information on that. In the meantime have a great day and again my number is 555-1231."

That voice mail is less than a minute. In fact, I was able to read that slowly and clearly in forty seconds. It was short and sweet and right to the point. Now don't forget to update your contact management and set a date for the next touch.

E-mail is especially important. Some people will respond to e-mail but will not take a phone call. However, keep it short, check your spelling, and make sure it is not sent as part of a group mailing. Touching is about building a relationship with individuals, and if they think you are sending the same message to fifty people at a time, your "touch" loses its impact. Here is an example of an effective e-mail touch:

> *Hi Sally,*
>
> *Roger Carnes with Executive Catering. Attached are our new hot lunch and boxed lunch menus. I wanted you to have these just in case you decide to give us a try sometime soon. As I mentioned when I talked to you a couple of months ago, we would love to have your business, and anytime you are ready to give us a try, please do not hesitate to let me know.*
>
> *In the meantime, have a great day.*
>
> *Roger*

Now update your contact management file and schedule the next touch.

Handwritten notes are an outstanding way to brand yourself with prospects, particularly with people who like to build relationships with their customers and vendors. You can really "Wow" some people by sending a handwritten personal message. Here's an example:

> *Angie:*
>
> *Thanks again for taking the time to talk to me last week. I know how busy you are during your peak season. As I said when we spoke, we would love the chance to do business with your company, so please feel free to call if there is anything we can do to be of assistance.*
>
> *Jerry*

I promise that a short, legible handwritten note to a prospective customer, hand addressed with a first class postage stamp and your business card neatly tucked inside, will get opened ninety-nine percent of the time. And while your prospects may only glance at the message and then pitch it, for those thirty seconds or so, you were registered in their head.

Using a stamp instead of a postage meter can really catch the prospect's eye. Most people don't pitch unopened mail with a first class stamp on it. Our curiosity gets the best of us.

Product or marketing brochures take on a whole new meaning when you take a fine tip felt maker and write a personal message on it. For example:

> *New product we're just introducing. Feel free to call if you would like any additional information.*
>
> *Jill*

Staple your business card to the piece or tuck it inside and either mail it or drop if off at the front desk of their company with your prospect's name on the envelope. It's one more "flirting" opportunity. And who knows, this one might be the one that piques their interest enough to give you a call.

Articles of interest are always big winners. Find an article on anything from the value of wearing headsets with cell phones to what colors on office walls motivate employees or tips on how to keep an office healthy during flu season.

The article's topic is irrelevant as long as it's generic and with broad appeal to business people. Resist sending articles specifically about your products or services. To the prospect, such information may not be as interesting as an article on what new college grads are looking for when job hunting.

Make copies of the article and handwrite personal messages to the recipient anywhere you can find space to write. For example:

> *Lisa, interesting article on colors in the workplace. Thought you might enjoy a copy. Who would have guessed that "orange" could positively impact stress?*
>
> *Barry*

Personally focused articles also can get you some real recognition from a prospect; just make sure you have your information correct. Here is an example.

Let's assume you had a brief meeting with Eric. He was not open to changing vendors at that time but has agreed to "keep you in mind." You are committed to going after the account, and Eric is in your touching program.

When you were in his office, you spent a couple of minutes discussing his antique German Beer Stein collection, as he had several pieces on display. You documented that information in your contact management file. Several weeks later you went online and searched for information on that subject.

You found an article about an elderly gentleman living on the East Coast who had the largest German Beer Stein collection in North America. The article also had some facts about the where he had traveled to find them. You print it, read it again, and then write Eric the following message on the article:

Eric:

Found this article about antique Beer Stein collections and thought you might want to have a copy. I was so impressed with your collection.

Enjoy!

Don

If Eric is an avid collector he may already have information about the elderly man's collection. In fact, he may have visited him and saw it first hand. That's not important. The fact that you remembered Eric was a collector and you took the time to send him an article on the subject will generally make a very positive impression.

Let me remind you one more time about the importance of documenting every touch in contact management. That documentation is tracking *who* you touched, *when* you touched, *how* you touched, and *when* you will touch again. ***This documentation is the key to your Touching Program's success.***

Imagine leaving a voice mail message in January, sending an article of interest in March, an e-mail invitation to your company open house in May, and a new product brochure in July with a personal message written on the cover. And, you've done the same with seventy-five to one hundred target accounts. This is what Superstar Sales Professionals do that sets them apart in competitive situations.

If you have one hundred prospects you want to touch once every eight weeks, that equates to less than thirteen touches per week. By allocating a two-hour block of time every other week, you only need to do twenty-five touches during that time to stay current. And think about how much of your touching you can do from home at night or on weekends instead of during peak selling times. I can't think of any valid excuse for any salesperson not having a successful Touching Program other than lack of discipline.

Take an evening at home and write ten personal messages on articles of interest, send ten e-mail messages, and the next day at the office you only have five calls or voice mails to complete. Now your Touching Program is done for two more weeks.

As I mentioned when we started this chapter, The Touching Program is not about skill; it's about discipline. It's making sure the people you want to do business with *know who you are.*

A number of years ago I was in St. Louis on business. Dinner with the client and his Vice President of sales at a well-known local Italian restaurant was also on the agenda.

When we arrived at the restaurant, it was packed. The hostess informed Jerry, my client, that without a reservation, the wait would be two hours for a table. A big convention was in town, and restaurants were especially busy that evening.

Jerry said to the lady taking reservations, "Would it make any difference if I told you that Tony (who owned the restaurant) and I were good friends and I eat here often? We're not with the convention." She promptly told Jerry there was nothing she could do and he would have to place his name on the list and wait his turn.

A couple of minutes later a tall gentleman walked by. He and Jerry shook hands, and then embraced. Jerry then introduced me to Tony, the restaurant's owner. Within five minutes we were seated and Tony had sent over a bottle of wine.

After an enjoyable dinner and business conversation I said to Jerry, "Tomorrow I am going to present business development sales training to your salespeople. Would you mind, Jerry, if I told the group how we were able to get this table so quickly tonight? There's a great sales message here."

Jerry did not mind at all but wanted to know more about the message. So I explained:

> **"Jerry, most people would say that we got this table so quickly tonight because you knew Tony. I disagree. I believe we got this table not because you knew Tony, but because Tony knew you."**

In sales, it's not who *you* know, but rather *who knows you.* The Touching Program is your way as a Superstar Sales Professional to make sure your prospects *know who you are.*

Key Points

➠ Allocate two hours, every two weeks, to keep your Touching Program up to date.

➠ Your Touching Program is not about skill; it's about discipline.

➠ You must have access to a computer-based contact management program for your Touching Program to be successful.

➠ Put prospects into your Touching Program funnel because:

    ➠ (a) They have the potential to be a good account or sale at some point in time, but right now there is no need and/or money.

    ➠ (b) They are doing business with a competitor and not open to changing or making a comparison at this time.

➠ As a salesperson, you must make sure your prospects remember you.

➠ Never put a prospect in a Touching Program at the first sign of resistance; rather, do so only after you have done everything you could, short of high pressure, to turn things around in your favor.

➠ Do not touch too frequently. Every six to eight weeks is generally enough for them to remember who you are.

➠ Do not ask prospects to respond to any of your touches unless they chose to do so.

➠ The objective to a successful Touching Program is branding you.

➠ Use postage stamps when sending handwritten notes or brochures rather than postage metered stamps. It catches the prospect's attention.

➠ There is no valid excuse for any salesperson not to have a successful Touching Program other than lack of discipline.

➠ In sales, it's not who *you* know, but rather *who knows you*.

CHAPTER 9

Listening and Asking Good Questions

Now we're in the door. We've done everything right, from the first attempt to reach the prospect all the way through meticulous management of our Touching Program. We have earned the opportunity to meet with the potential customer.

At this point, our ability to gain the customer's trust and interest is key to our success. Starting out by telling them all about our company, our products and services, and why they should do business with us is *not* the way to make that happen. In fact, doing so will often cause you to quickly *lose* their interest.

The most common mistakes salespeople make when meeting with a prospective customer for the first time are:

- They talk too much.

- They don't ask enough good questions.

- They fail to uncover true needs.

Talking Too Much

All salespeople must have a good understanding of the products and services they offer. But realize that most customers are not interested in hearing about products or services until they feel the salesperson fully understands *their* needs. Even so, far too many salespeople start a first meeting with a prospective customer by talking too much about what they have to offer.

Superstar Sales Professionals take a different approach. They encourage the prospective customer to talk while they listen.

Our goal should be to make our prospects feel that we are there to **learn**, not educate. Encourage them to tell you anything and everything they might want you to know about their particular situation or needs. And take notes! This is great way to demonstrate you are listening and taking nothing for granted.

If you see a solution to a problem or a need, or if you hear what we often refer to as a "buying signal," don't be too quick to talk about it. Be patient; your time will come. If you move in too quickly you might find you've misinterpreted what the prospect was saying and end up looking somewhat foolish. Here's an example of what I mean:

> *Prospect: "Having dependable, next day delivery is a very important issue to us."*

> *Salesperson: "That's not a problem. We do that every day. We have fourteen trucks delivering all over the city starting at 7:00 a.m. in the morning, Monday through Friday."*

> *Prospect: "Well our current supplier does the same thing. In fact, they even offer a Saturday morning service if the order is over a certain amount."*

In this example, our salesperson thought he heard a "buying signal" and jumped in too soon to talk about what his company offered. Did he look a little foolish? You bet. He assumed his next day delivery service was something the prospect was not currently getting and would like to have.

Asking Good Questions

Earlier in this book we mentioned that selling was not about telling but rather about asking. In the scenario just highlighted, our salesperson might have learned more if he had addressed the prospect's comments by asking a question instead of pitching his delivery service.

To quote Stephen Covey, author of the best-selling book *Seven Habits of Highly Effective People:*

> *"Don't listen to just formulate a response. Listen to truly understand your customer's specific circumstances. Don't assume you know what they want or what concerns them."*

So what could our salesperson have asked if he had been focused more on listening and asking rather then telling? Here's an example:

> Prospect: *"Having dependable, next day delivery is a very important issue to us."*

> Salesperson: *"I certainly understand. We hear the same thing from many of our customers. Melissa, how often are you not able to get your supplies delivered the day after an order is placed?"*

> Prospect: *"Our current supplier is pretty good about getting things here the next day. Once in awhile they run late, and that puts us in a bind, but you can't control weather or traffic."*

Now our salesperson knows that singing the praises of *his* next day delivery service is not necessarily the hot button he needs to push to impress the prospect. He needs to ask more questions and probe further to find something he has to offer that might be of value and interest.

Gain a Clear Understanding of the Prospect's Needs and Objectives

Developing effective probing skills is very important in solution-based selling. If a prospective customer is to decide *you* are the person to do business with, he or she must feel that you understand his or her needs and priorities. And while knowing what someone wants is important, it's not as important as knowing *why* he or she wants it. Here's an example:

> Prospect: *"When we look at office furniture for the new building, seating is going be at the top of the priority list. It's our call center's number one complaint."*

> Salesperson: *"Carlos, what specific complaints are you hearing from the call center staff?"*

> Prospect: *"They say the chairs they have now are hard to adjust and don't provide enough back support. Our people are stuck in their chairs for hours when the call center is busy, and if their backs are hurting they're probably not as productive as they could be."*

Now our salesperson not only knows that the prospect needs new chairs, but also what will be most important in the buying decision and why. She probed for clarification and complete understanding, and it worked.

Probing for Clarification

Some salespeople are uncomfortable probing. They say they feel they are being "nosey." In their minds they believe they have no right to ask the customer probing questions, and the customer might tell them "that's none of your business." While the chances of the prospect actually saying that are rare, the salesperson still feels it *could* happen so he or she simply avoids asking probing questions.

These salespeople often feel subservient to the customer and do not place enough value on their own professional expertise and knowledge. These are the same salespeople who struggle to be successful. Their customers often view them as order takers and customer service reps instead of salespeople. As a result, their clients don't value them or seek their advice and expertise.

Probing for additional information and clarification tells your customers that you are listening and interested in knowing and understanding their needs. How can we provide solutions to customers if we don't uncover problems and needs? As Stephen Covey said: ***"Don't assume you know what they want or what concerns them."***

How to Probe and Ask Good Questions

When probing, you need to ask open-ended questions. Use closed-ended questions only when you want a "yes," "no," or one word answer.

Open-ended questions encourage dialog. Such questions often begin with Who, What, Where, When, How, and sometimes (with caution) Why.

Why do you need to use caution with "why" questions? Sometimes prospects can view "why" questions as challenging or adversarial. If you're not careful, "why" questions can sound harsh. However, you can always rephrase a "why" question as follows. Instead of, *"Why do you feel so strongly about that?"* you can say, *"Share with me why you feel so strongly about that?"* The latter is much less challenging.

Here are some examples of open-ended probing questions:

> *"John, what do you see as the number one objective in renovating your sales department?"*

> *"If today were the day you were going to replace your color copier, what would you want the new one to do or to have that would different from your 2230 model?"*

> *"Dan, if you could, how would you change the program you currently have?"*

Conversely, closed-ended questions often limit conversation, because the customer can easily answer them with a "yes," "no," or one word answer. Such questions often start with Do, Is, Are, Can, Does, Will, Have, Had, Could, Would, and Should.

Here are some examples of closed-ended questions:

> *"John, do you have a primary objective in renovating your sales department?"*

> *"If today were the day you were going to replace your color copier, would you want anything to be added that you don't have now?"*

> *"Dan, if it were possible, is there anything you would change with the program you currently have?"*

Another mistake I see salespeople make is asking a question and then providing multiple choice answers, as in:

> *"John, what do you see as the number one objective in renovating your sales department? Is it productivity or appearance, or do you need more space?"*

While using closed-ended questions and questions followed by multiple choice answers is not the most effective way to get a customer to open up and talk, many salespeople ask such questions anyway. Why? "Fear of the Silence."

Asking an open-ended question and then saying nothing until the customer responds can be awkward and uncomfortable for the non-skilled salesperson. However, to Superstar Sales Professionals, it's as natural as breathing because they have practiced it to perfection.

How to Ask Questions Like a Superstar Sales Professional

First, **listen**. Truly listen to what your prospect is saying rather than thinking about what you are going to say. Listen, and then identify the key words or key message you just heard. Next, ask yourself what additional information you would like to know. Finally, ask an open-ended question. Here are some examples:

> **Prospect:** *"Our **CEO is adamant** about the **image we project** when advertising in magazines."*

The key words or key messages are in bold print. The unskilled salesperson would probably start talking right now about how to project a good image in their ads and all the different ways to do so. However, the Superstar Sales Professional will ask a question to gain further clarification. The question could be any of the following:

> *"Nancy, why is your CEO so adamant about the company's image?"*

Or,

> *"What is the image your CEO wants to project in magazine advertising?"*

Or,

"How does he feel about the image your ads are projecting now?"

Here's another example of a prospect response. This time the keys words are not bolded, so see if you can determine what they are.

Prospect: *"We need a lot of flexibility with the way we're growing."*

If you chose "flexibility" and "growing," you are correct. Your open-ended questions could be any of the following:

"Wayne, specifically what kind of flexibility would you need?"

Or,

"What are your growth expectations for the next six to twelve months?"

Or,

"What about the system you have now is not as flexible as you need?"

In order to truly uncover their prospects' needs, sales professionals must learn to listen and ask good questions. And while it's not difficult, doing so takes practice and discipline. In the end, however, mastering this skill does more in getting the customer to *want* to buy from you than anything else you can do.

When customers *want* to buy from you, it's almost always because they feel you truly understand their needs and you can and will do what you say you can do. This relationship helps much in overcoming price and existing relationship objections.

Once you have identified their true needs, you can present what you have to offer with confidence and full knowledge that it's a good fit, and why. The result is that closing the sale becomes easier, and winning sales happens more frequently.

Closing sales is actually a very small part of the sales process when you have done a good job of uncovering needs. Additionally, you will have an easier time addressing price issues when you know what your customers need to accomplish their overall objective.

For a minute, let's go back to Carlos, who wanted good chairs for his call center staff. Because our salesperson knows what the complaints have been and what quality chairs can accomplish for Carlos and his staff, she is better prepared to address price.

If what Carlos has budgeted for new chairs will not get him the quality he wants to satisfy his call center needs, our salesperson has the information she needs to effectively address the issue. Let's look at how that might flow:

> *"Carlos, to give your staff the adjustability and the back support they need, we'll risk losing some of that if we go to a less expensive chair. What are the chances you would consider spending a little more to get the chairs you really need?"*

Whether Carlos agrees to spend more or not, our salesperson would not have had a chance to negotiate the price without the knowledge of *why* Carlos needed the quality chairs. Without that knowledge, most salespeople would take the path of least resistance and lower the price of the chair.

The Superstar Sales Professional, however, would not. The Superstar Sales Professional would first attempt to convince Carlos to increase the budget, or, if all else fails, present him with a less expensive chair. The Superstar Sales Professional is always focused on solution-based selling, not sales for the sake of sales.

A Real-Life Superstar Sales Professional Example

A number of years ago my husband Earl and I decided to convert our screened-in deck into a sunroom we could use year round. Living in Ohio with cold winters, we usually experience five to six months out of the year when the deck is unusable

Avid wild bird lovers for years, we had attracted some beautiful birds to our feeders and watering stations at the edge of the woods behind our home. The deck provided us with a most spectacular view, which we were missing during the cold months.

Once we made the decision to move forward, we started looking for contractors to do the job. We visited the Spring Home and Garden Show and selected three companies we wanted to talk to and get estimates from.

Tuesday morning the first salesperson arrived. He was dressed in a blue uniform and carried a tape measure and a clipboard. After quickly shaking hands with Earl and me, he marched immediately to the deck and started taking measurements and spouting off questions.

"Where do you want the door opening?"

"How are you planning to finish off the floor?"

"Are you looking for a single door or double sliding doors?"

"Do you want any electrical outlets in this room?"

"Do you want the glass all the way to the floor or just to chair height?"

He was shooting questions at us like a Gestapo Interrogator. I was about to stop him when Earl gave me "that look" he gives me from time to time that says, *"No, you are not going to give him sales coaching."* But that's exactly what I wanted to do.

I wanted to tell him that if we had all the answers to his questions, we would have just worked up a "to do" list and asked him to price them one at a time. We were not the experts; he was. How much did we know about building a room on the back of the house?

That afternoon our second salesperson came to visit. When I answered the door he was standing there with a forty-pound book in his hands that seemed two-feet thick. I knew I was in trouble when he asked, *"Could we just sit at the dining room table for a few minutes? There are a few things I would like to show you."*

For over an hour he rambled on and on, picture after picture, about how they built their rooms and how the glass had green stuff heated in it so the sun would not hurt your furniture and how they had ninety-nine different finishes for your trim and how they had a four hundred year warranty and how now was the time to move forward so we can get the Garden Show sale special and on and on and on. I thought he would never stop talking. Unfortunately, I could not stop him because Earl kept giving me "that look."

Earl has much more patience than I do, and he prefers to let salespeople do their thing. Then he just scratches them off the list.

Wednesday morning our third salesperson, Winston, arrived. When we greeted him at the door, he had a big smile and a small briefcase. After a few minutes of the pleasantries about our two Chihuahuas and our great view of the woods in the back, he asked to see the deck. He walked around the area, took a couple of measurements, and then he looked at Earl and said, *"Okay, you folks have a really nice screened in deck here. Tell me why you want to change it into an all seasons' room?"*

Yes! Finally a salesperson who was asking us what we wanted to accomplish.

After we rambled on for a few minutes about our wild birds and the woods, Winston said he wanted to walk out back for a minute. Now this was March and a bit chilly, but he walked around the yard and looked back at the house several times before coming back in. When he stepped back inside he said, *"Winnie and Earl, if I have this right, what you are saying to me is that this room conversion is about a view. Am I correct?"*

Yes! Winston understood.

For the next hour he talked about angles, the positioning of glass, finishing off ceilings and doorways and trim, all while continuing to focus on making sure that nothing obscured the view, which was our number one objective. And because he knew that piece of information, he even suggested cathedral ceilings with skylights to let in more sun in the winter and a spectacular view of the sky in the evenings.

When it was time to talk about price, he asked if he could have five minutes at the kitchen table to work out the figures. We gave him a cup of coffee and moved to the living room to allow him to do his work undisturbed. During that entire time I said to myself over and over: "I really hope he gives us a price we can afford because this is the person we *want to do business with."*

Winston had done a terrific job of listening, probing for clarification, and getting us to *want* to hear what he had to offer. He had uncovered the need, provided the solution, and won the sale.

As I write this chapter, I am using my laptop on a small portable computer stand and sitting inside my new sunroom. I see a Carolina Wren perched on the deck railing, and a huge Robin eating the last of the ripened crab apples on a tree. Two Chickadees are pecking away at sunflower seeds they've pulled from a nearby feeder, and no less than half a dozen Downey Woodpeckers are on the suet racks that hang in the back

Thank you, Winston. You exemplify the term "Superstar Sales Professional."

Key Points

➡ Mistakes salespeople make when meeting with a prospective customer for the first time are:

    ➡ They talk too much.

    ➡ They don't ask enough good questions.

    ➡ They fail to uncover true needs.

➡ Make the prospect feel we are there to **learn**, not educate.

➡ Selling is not about telling, but rather about asking.

➡ Probing for clarification is the best way to gain a clear understanding of the prospect's needs and objectives.

➡ Open-ended questions encourage dialog and often begin with Who, What, Where, When, How . . . and with caution Why.

➡ Use closed-ended questions only when you want a "yes," "no," or one word answers.

➡ Closed-ended questions often limit conversation, because prospects can easily answer them with "yes," "no," or one word responses.

➡ Closed–ended questions often start with Do, Is, Are, Can, Does, Will, Have, Had, Could, Would, and Should.

➡ The Superstar Sales Professional is always focused on solution-based selling, not sales for the sake of sales.

CHAPTER 10

Drills for Skills

"Train hard; fight easy."
~George Foreman

When world famous boxing champion George Foreman beat Michael Moorer in 1994 to regain the heavyweight crown at age forty-five, he made history. No one believed that a forty-five-year-old boxer could win the title.

Later, during a press interview, someone asked Foreman what was the hardest part of the fight. Foreman replied that the fight had been easy—training for the fight had been the most difficult part. He said: "Train hard; fight easy."

The same concept applies to developing good selling skills. You must practice to develop the skills necessary to become a Superstar Sales Professional.

Drills for Skills

As a trainer, I know the value of practice. When I teach sales training, I often offer the attendees various ways to practice the skills we cover. The goal is to make the newly learned skills as natural as breathing. Here are some of the "Drills for Skills" I often suggest.

1. Practice in private:

Initially, most people are not comfortable making telephone prospecting calls if others are listening. So find a private office or area to practice your skills until you are comfortable with what you're doing and saying.

2. Tape record yourself often:

Record calls you make to prospects and customers, even if you only tape your end of the conversation. Later, listen to what you said and ask yourself the following:

- Did I sound confident, professional, important, or did I sound apologetic and too accommodating?

- How often did I probe for additional information and clarification versus using closed-ended questions that can end in "yes" or "no"?

- Did I listen and learn, or did I do too much of the talking?

3. Practice addressing objections:

Make a list of every objection you might confront in your business—everything from "We buy from Valley View and we're happy" to "Your price is too high."

Once you have completed a list of at least fifteen to twenty objections, write out how you might transition to an open-ended question for each one.

Next, record just the objections on your tape recorder, leaving five seconds blank in between each one. Rewind the tape, hit play, and then respond to each objection you hear with the open-ended question you had written.

Do this repeatedly until you know that if and when you actually hear one of the objections from a prospect or customer, your response will be as natural as brushing your teeth.

4. Ask who, what, when, where, how, and why:

Take any magazine or newspaper and read one sentence from any article. Then, see how many questions you can ask about what you've read that begins with one of the above highlighted words.

Here's an example:

Article sentence: "Congress hopes the bill will pass by the 15th."

Your questions:

- ❏ **Who** will the bill impact most?

- ❏ **What** is the bill about?

- ❑ **When** will they know if it passed?

- ❑ **Where** will they be casting the votes?

- ❑ **How** likely is it that it will pass?

- ❑ **Why** is the 15th so important?

When you practice allowing yourself to be inquisitive, you will listen better, ask good questions, and probe for clarification more confidently and competently with customers and prospects.

Play games with your peers. See how long you can keep a conversation going without using the words Do, Is, Are, Can, Will, Does, Have, Could, Would, and Should.

5. Set goals:

This is my favorite Drill for Skills: Get a piece of paper about the size of a business card, *right now.*

In the lower left hand corner put today's date. In the upper right hand corner put January 1, three years from now. Allow yourself the balance of the current year and two more years to reach your goal.

In the center of that piece of paper, in big bold print, write the amount of money you want to see on your W2 for the year ending the day before the January first date you have in the upper right hand corner.

Fold up the piece of paper, write "Keep" on the outside, and put it in your wallet. I promise, you will not get rid of that piece of paper until one of three things happen:

- You lose your wallet, but the Superstar Sales Professional will just replace that piece of paper with a new one.

- You quit and determine that being a Superstar Sales Professional is not for you.

- You make your goal and quickly replace your piece of paper with one that has a new goal.

The Superstar Sales Professional Always W.I.N.S.

In this book we have talked a lot about what a Superstar Sales Professional *is* and the skills these people must *master* to be successful. We've addressed the importance of discipline, attitude, and practice.

Yet, even with this knowledge, some people will reach the Superstar levels while others will not. Why? Beyond discipline, attitude, and practice, what's the final element to become a Superstar Sales Professional? Well, the Superstar Sales Professional *always* W.I.N.S. Here's what W.I.N.S. stands for:

Want:
You must want success and want it with a passion. You must want to be successful in sales and have the report card to back it up. Thinking you can make it, you should make it, or you need to make it is not enough. You have to want to become a Superstar Sales Professional or it won't happen.

Initiative:
Webster defines initiative as the first step in a process that, once taken, determines subsequent events. You have to get going to get there. That takes *Initiative*, and Superstar Sales Professionals have a lot of it.

Negativism:
You can't be a pessimist or a negative thinking person and still be a Superstar Sales Professional. You will have times when prospects are rude, you lose sales you were sure you were going to win, or your best customer decides to give their business to a competitor. Superstar Sales Professionals kick into gear and move forward, even in tough times.

Skill:
This is the most important letter in the acronym. Superstar Sales Professionals make things happen, win more often, and earn more money because they are *Skilled* professionals.

Good Luck and Good Selling!

Book Order Form

Phone: 1-866-372-2636 (Continental USA Only) OR **Phone:** 1-843-645-3770 (Have your credit card handy.)

Secure Online Ordering: www.arygroup.com

Fax Orders: 1-843-645-3771

How to Become a $uperstar $ales Professional:
Prospecting and Solution-Based Selling Skills for Business to Business Sales Professionals (ISBN 0-9-774659-4-2)

$18.95 US FUNDS / $23.00 CAN FUNDS

Orders of 15-24 books SAVE 10%. ($17.06 US / $20.70 CAN)

Orders of 25-49 books SAVE 15%. ($16.11 US / $19.55 CAN)

Orders of 50+ books SAVE 20%. ($15.16 US / $18.40 CAN)

Books _____ x $ _____ = _____

        + S & H   _____

      Order Total =   _____

*To receive quantity discount pricing, please call in your order to 1-866-372-2636 OR 1-843-645-3770.

Value of Order	S & H Charges:
$10 to $25	$5.25
$26 to $50	$6.00
$51 to $75	$7.00
$76 to $100	$8.00
$101 to $150	$9.00
$151 to $200	$10.00
$201 to $300	$15.00
$301 to $450	- see "Bulk Orders"

Bulk Orders: Shipping charges are calculated on bulk orders by the weight of the shipment and the distance it is being shipped. On bulk orders we suggest that you estimate shipping at 10% of your order; however, actual published shipping charges will be added to your total.

Name: _____

Company: _____

Address: _____

City: _____ State: ___ Zip: _____

Phone: _____ Email: (optional) _____

Name on card: _____

Card # _____ Exp date: _____

circle credit card

Feel free to contact the author with comments regarding the book:
Winnie Ary ~ email: winnie@arygroup.com
or visit www.arygroup.com